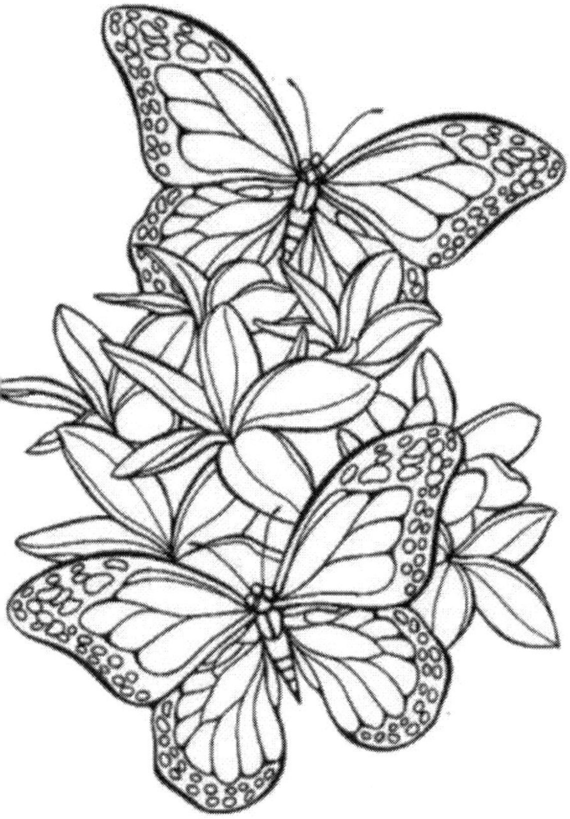

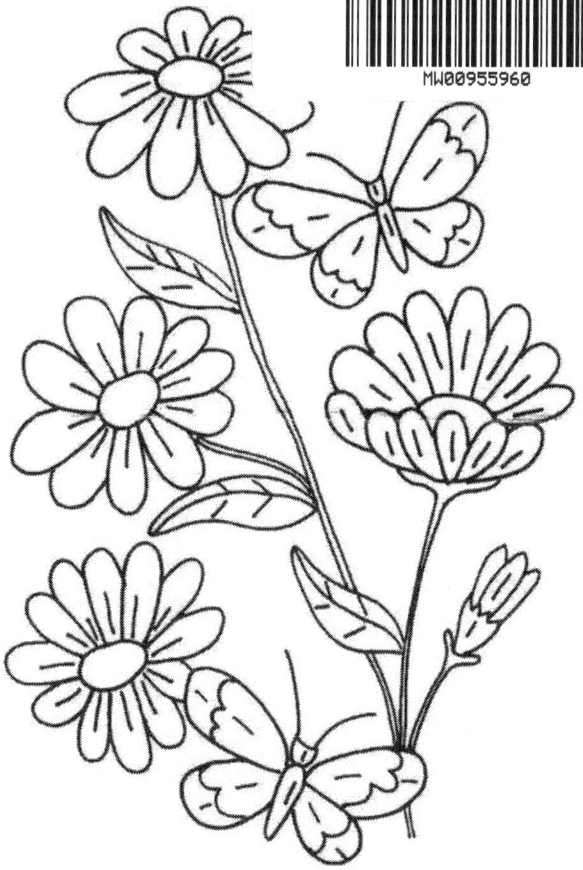

This Book Is Belong To

Name: ____________________

Phone: ____________________

Email: ____________________

Your Color Test Page Here

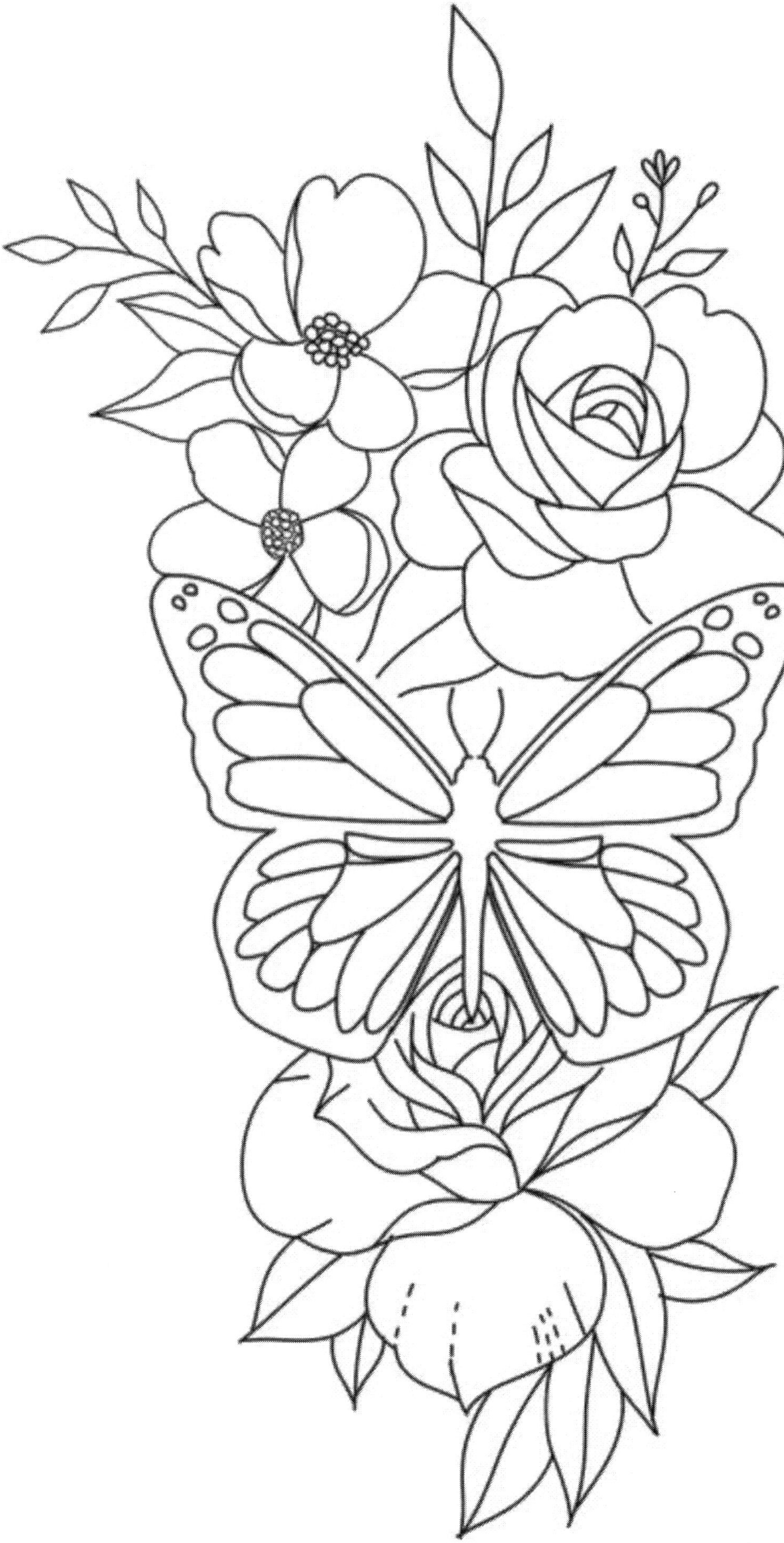

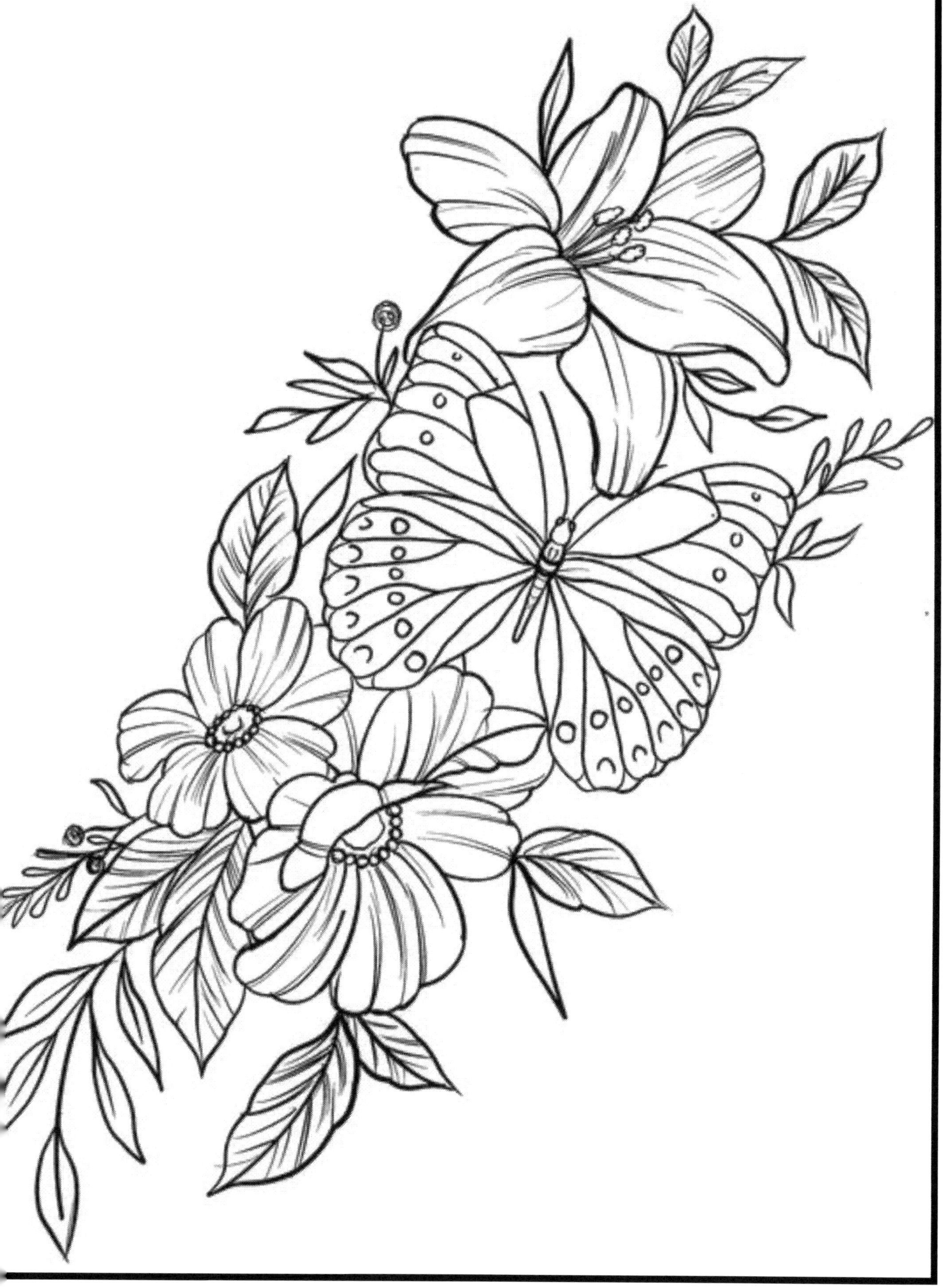

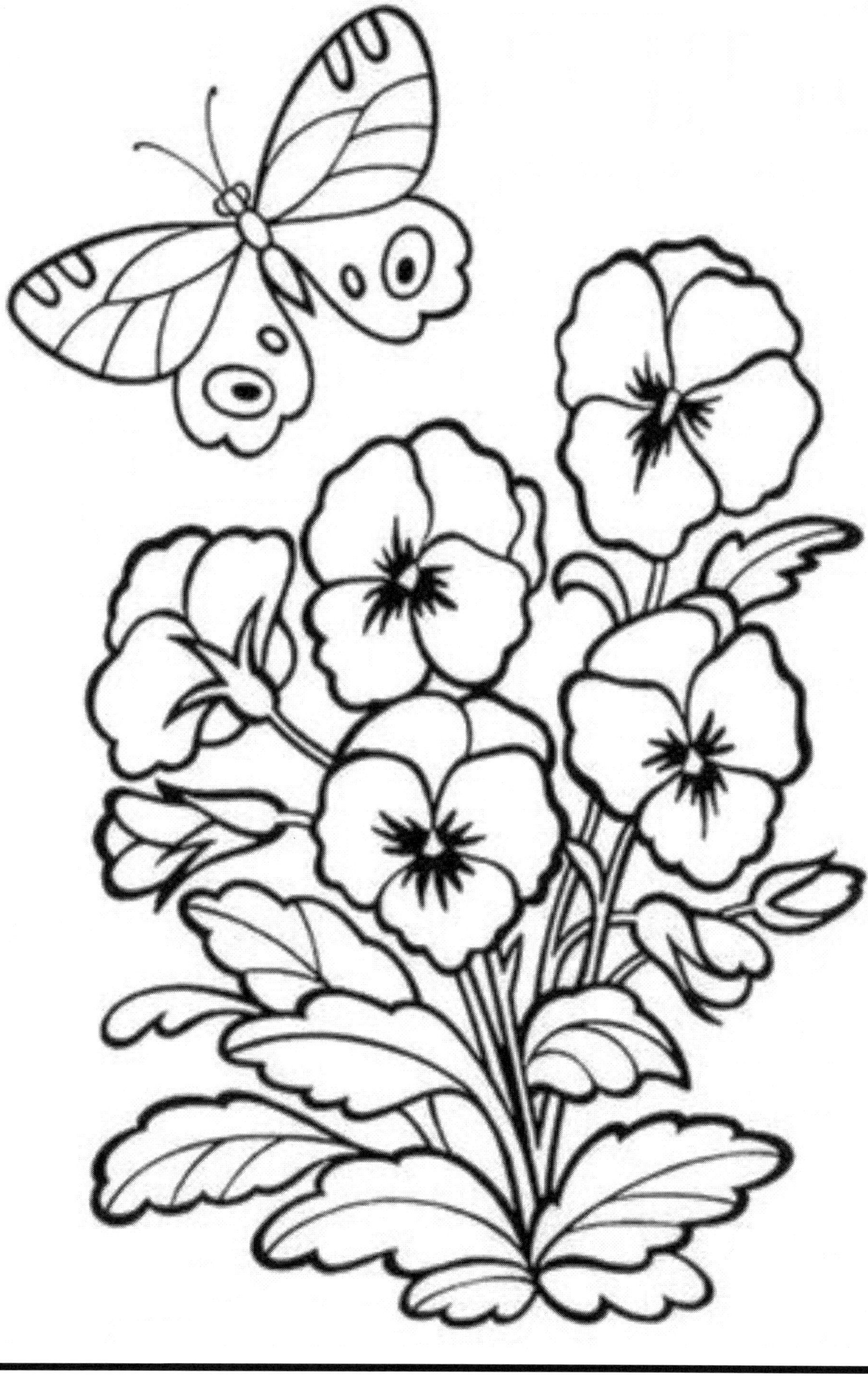

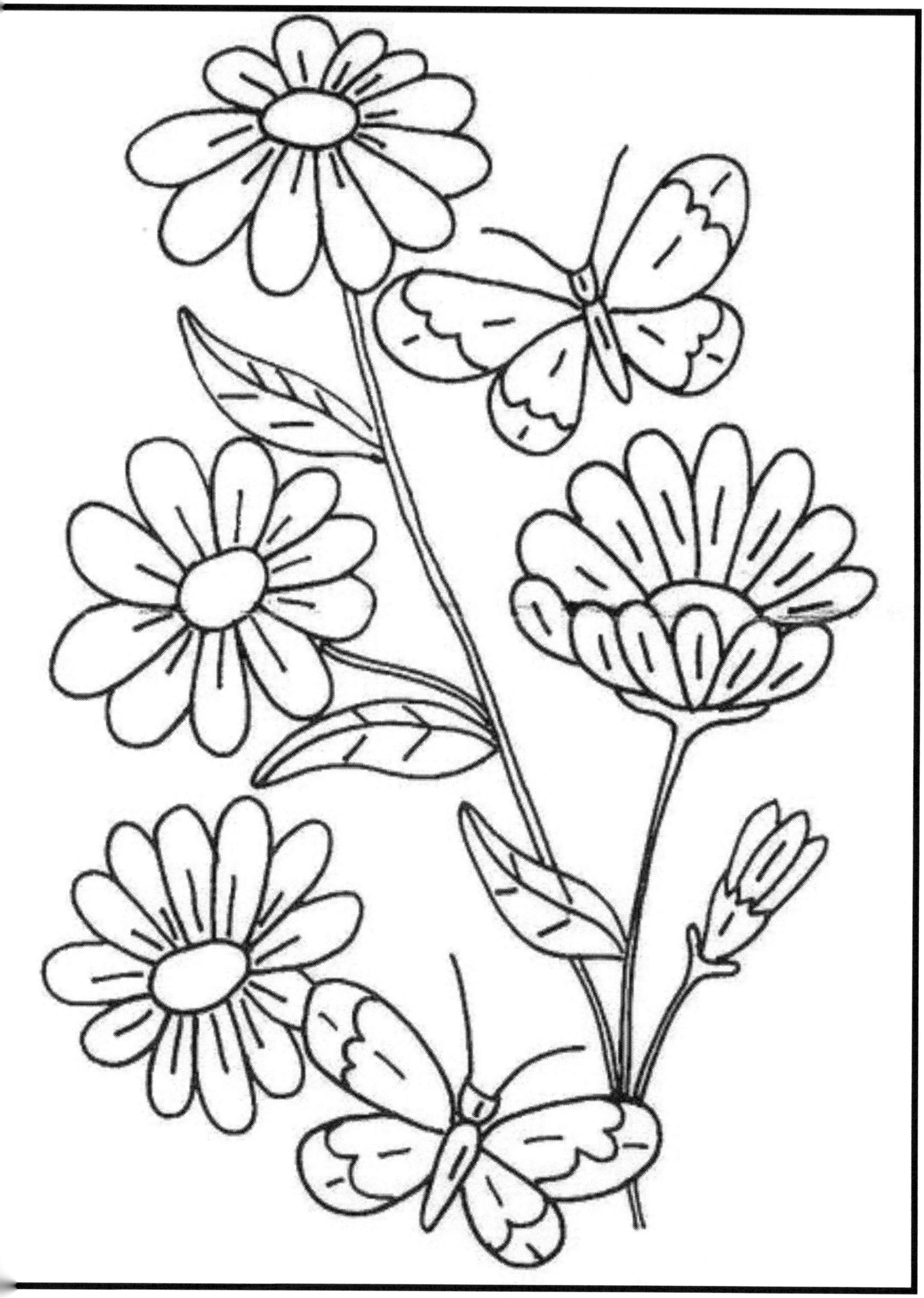

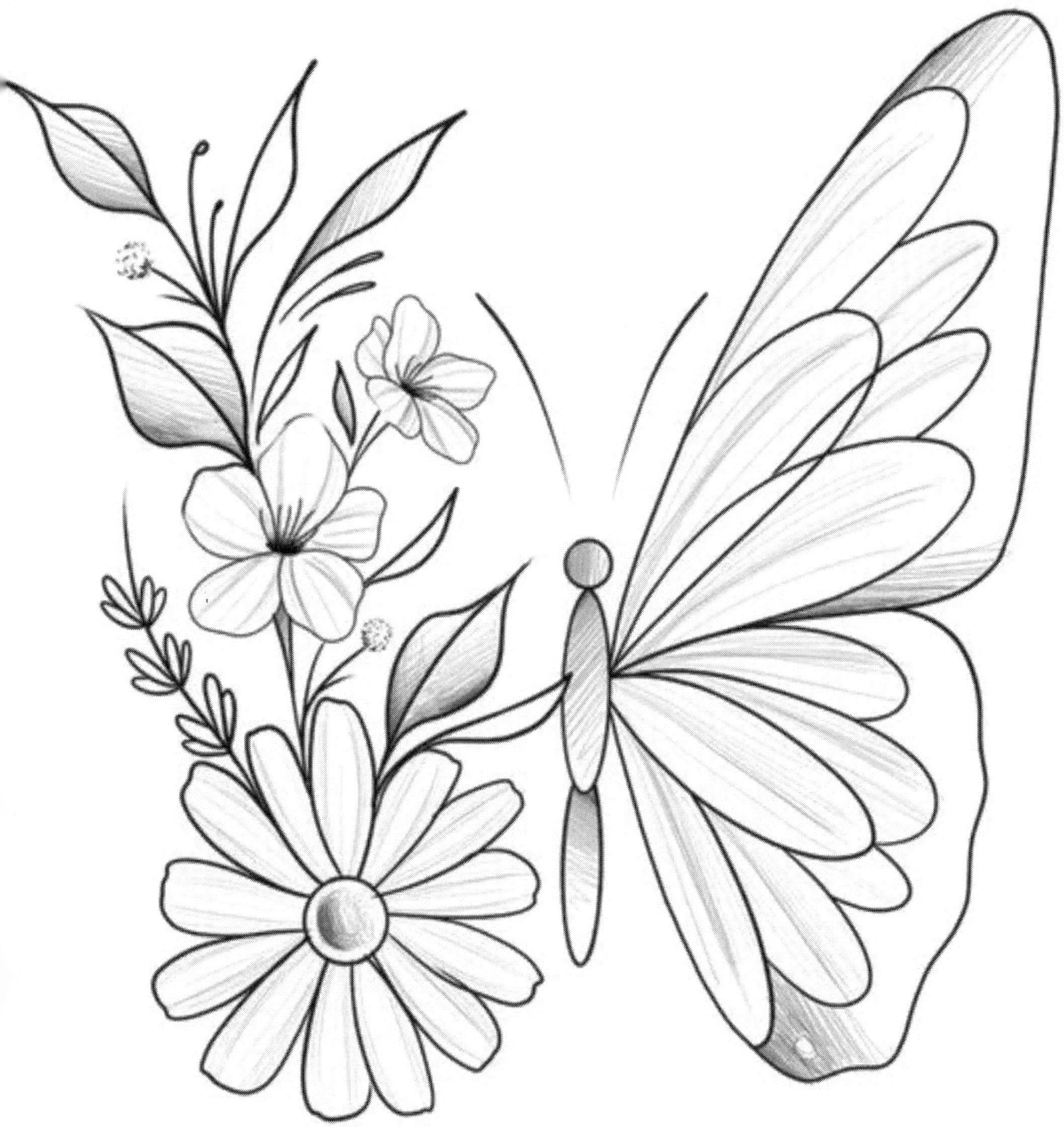

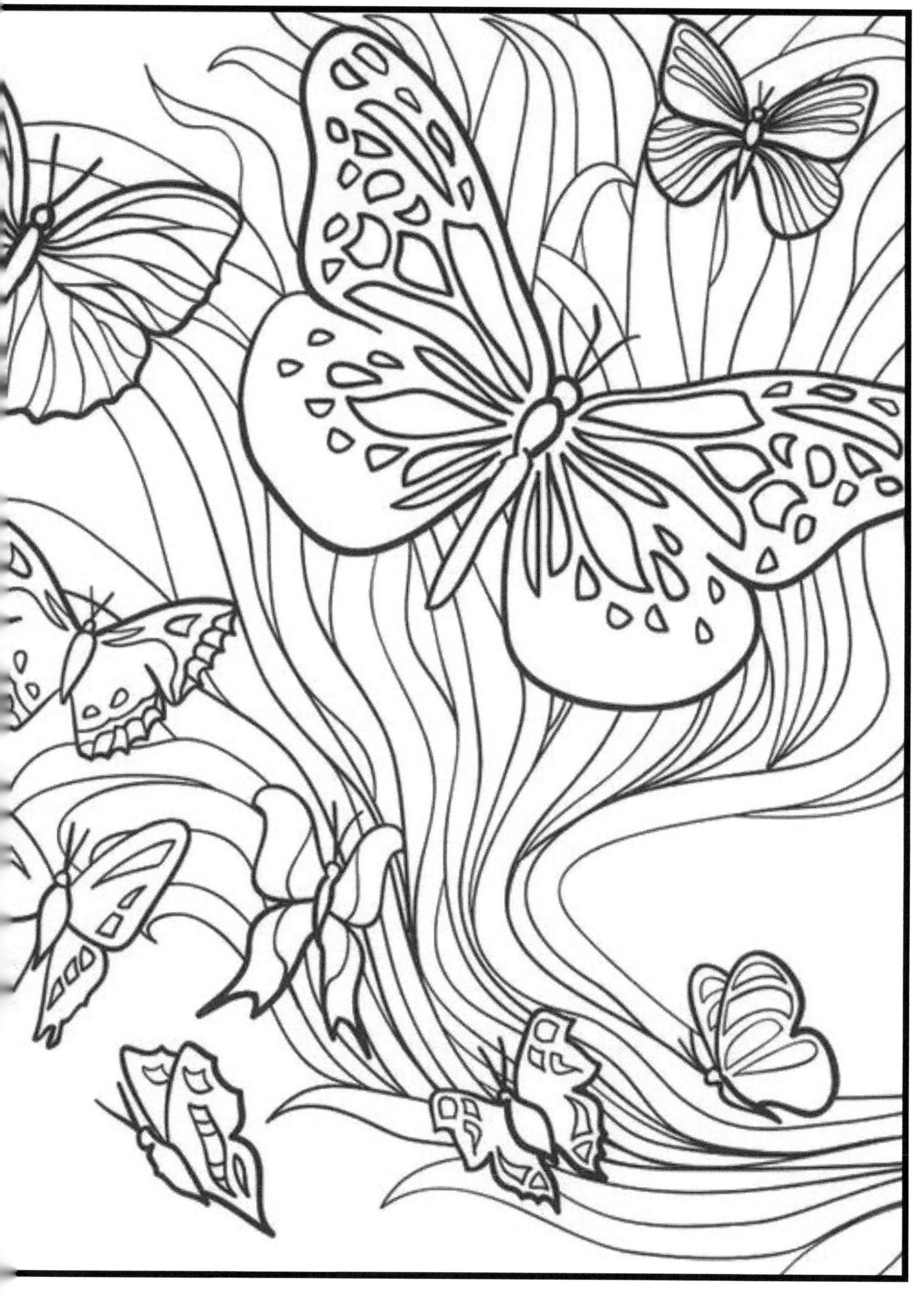

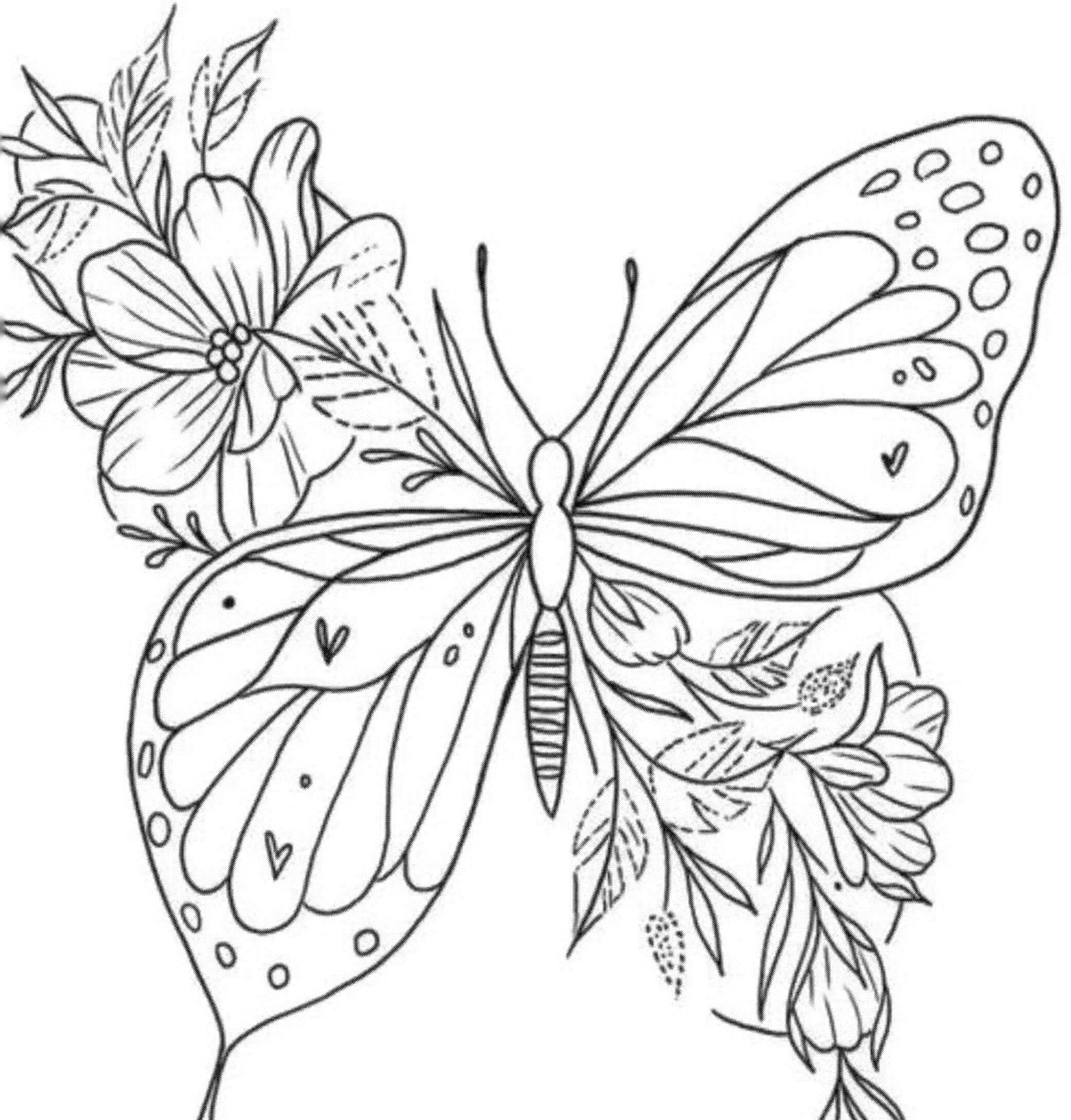

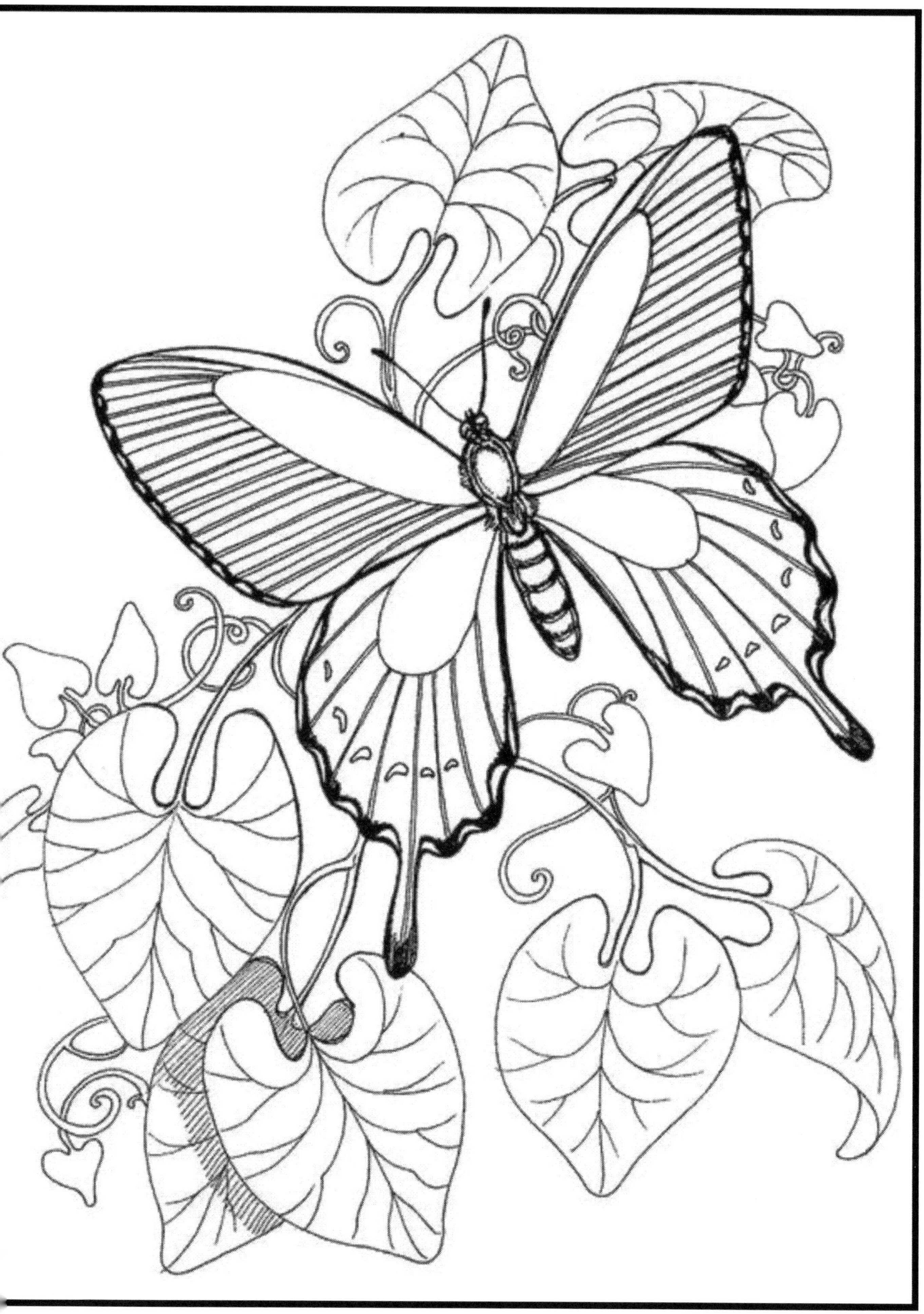

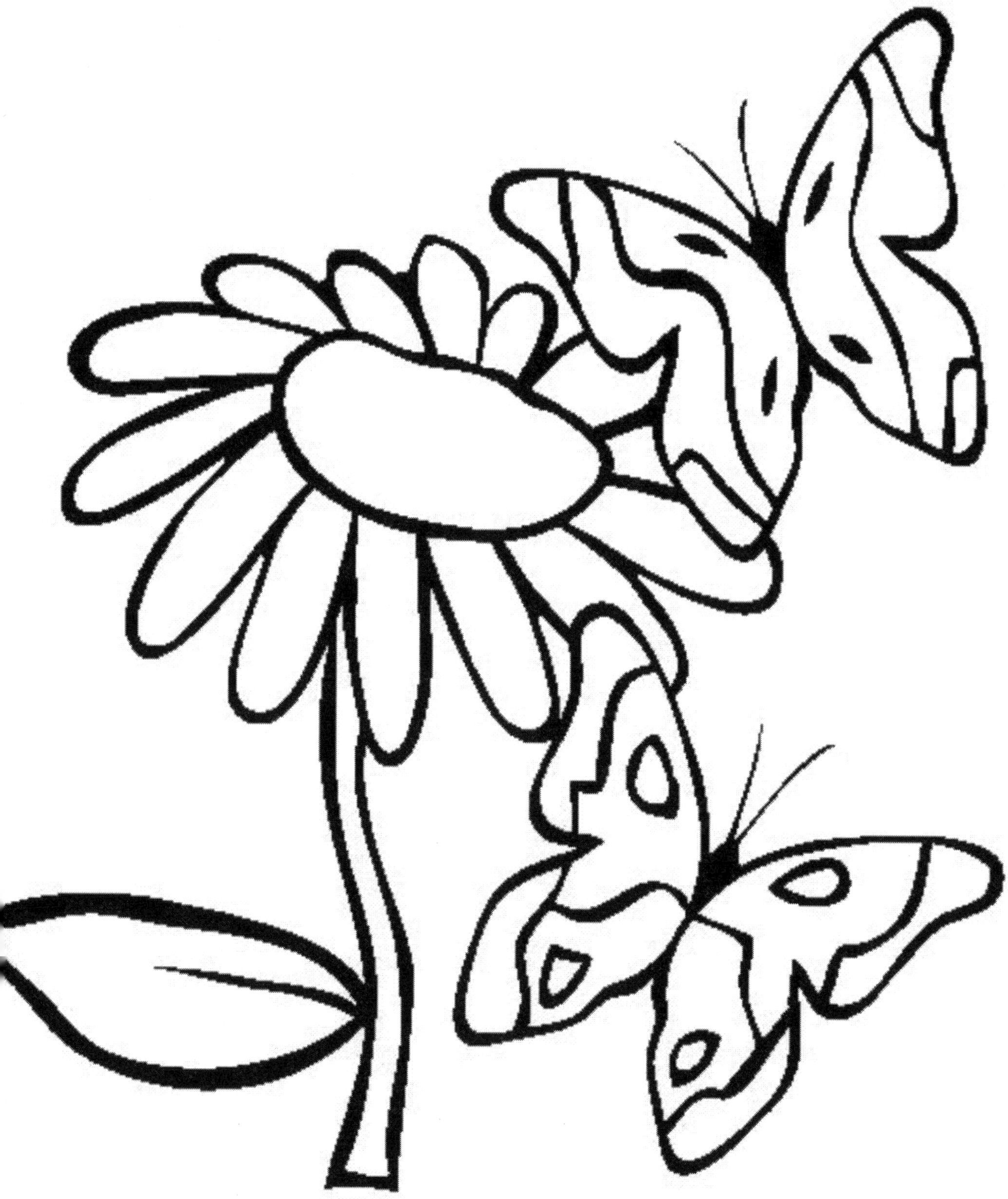

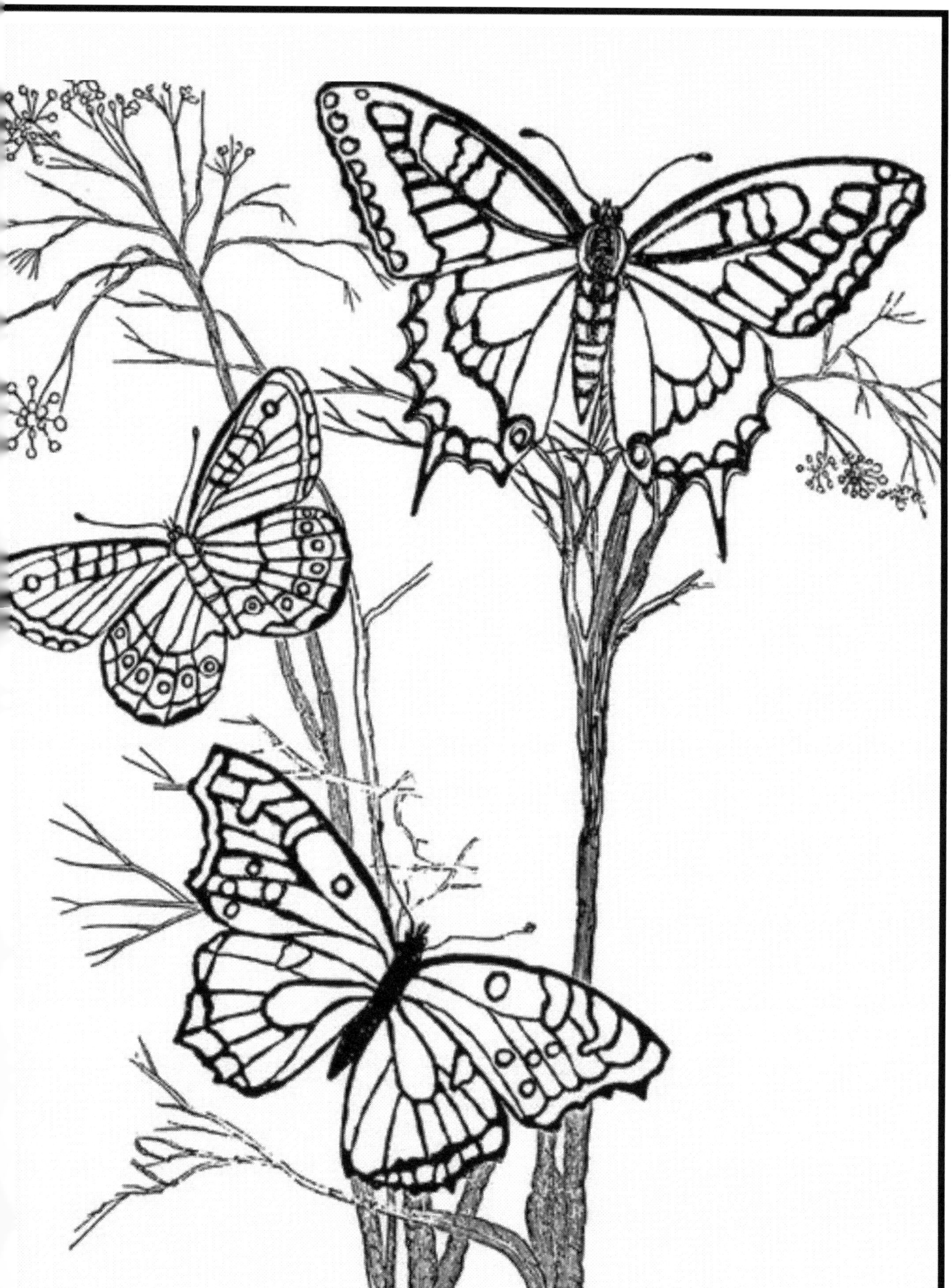

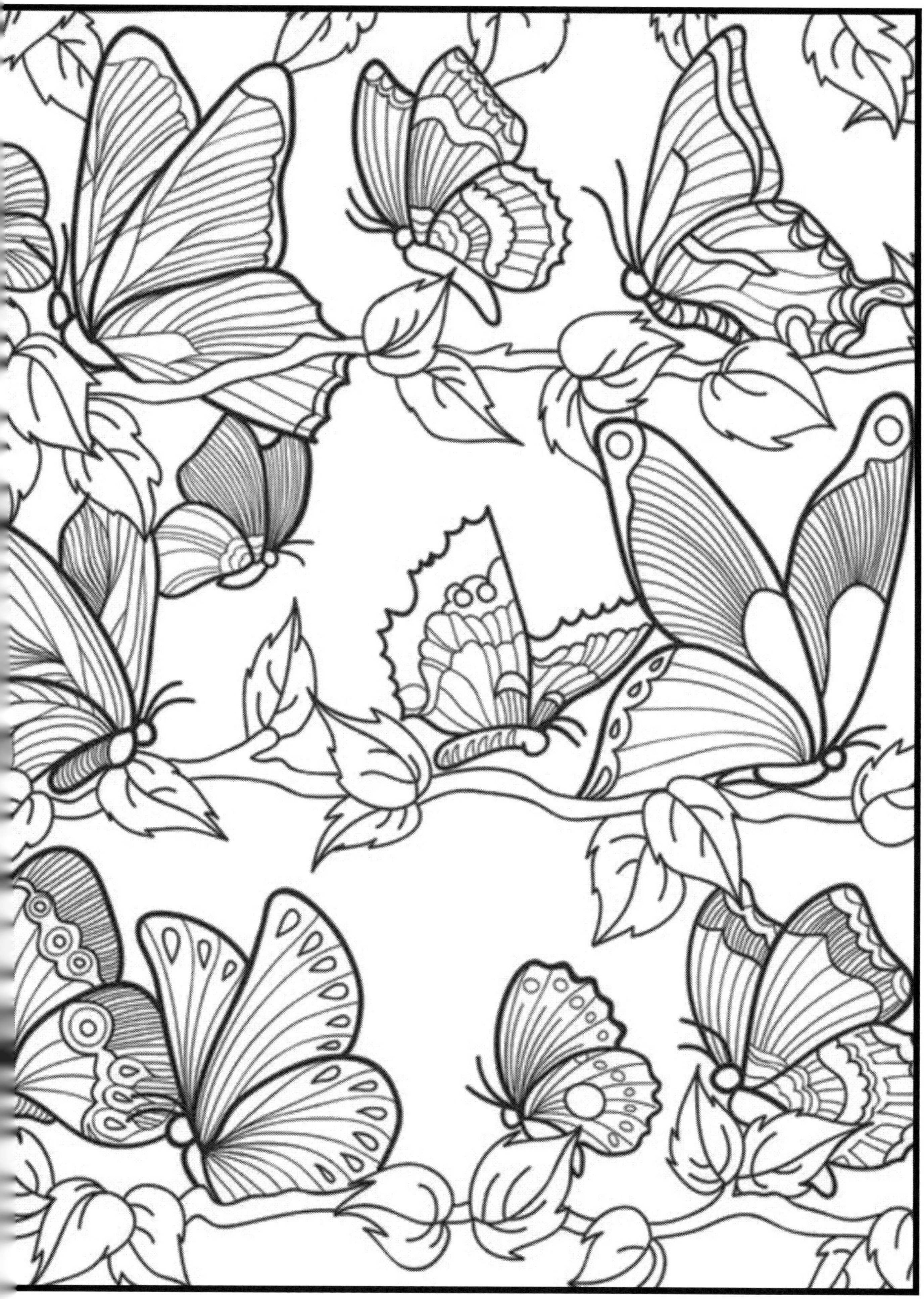

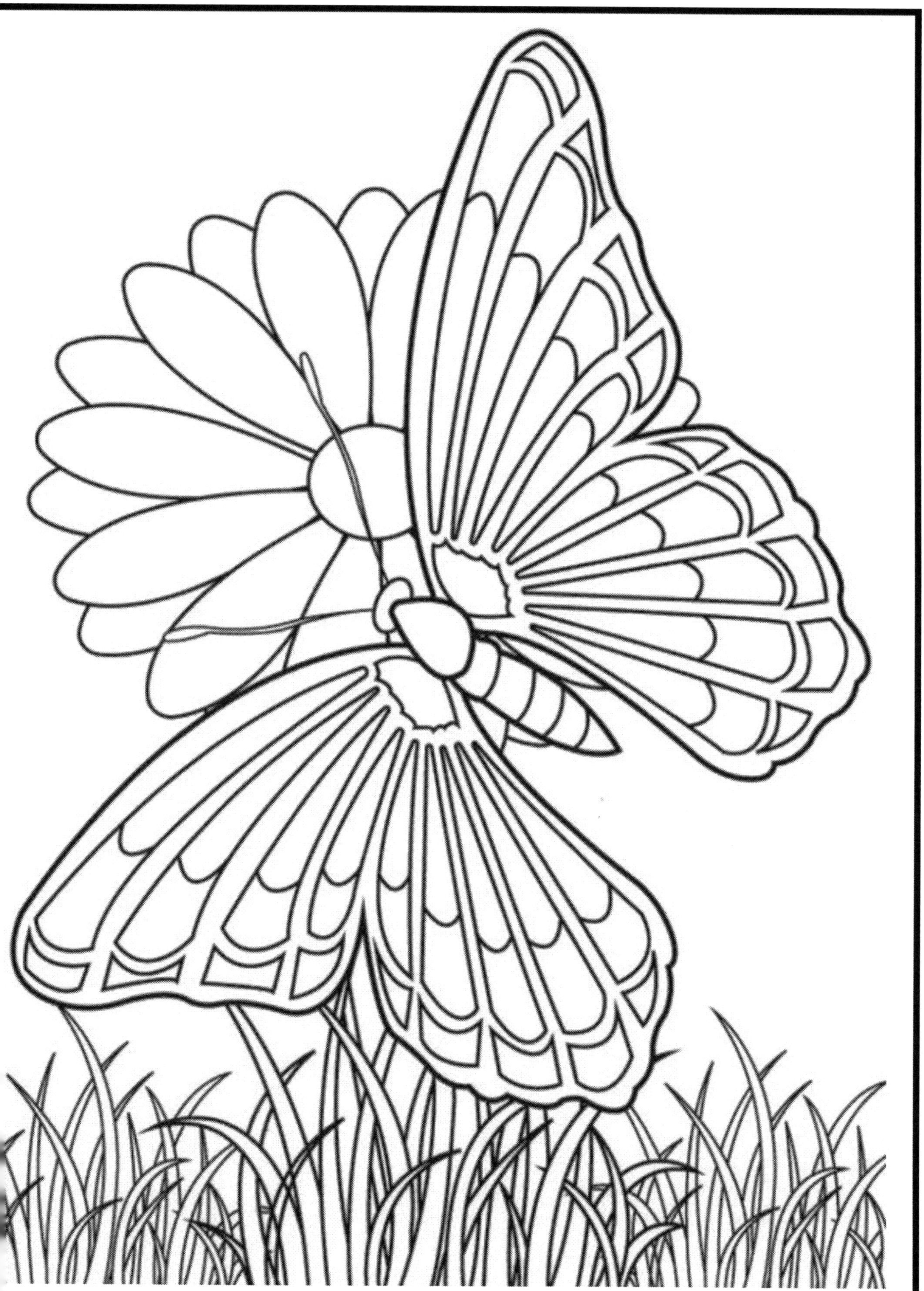

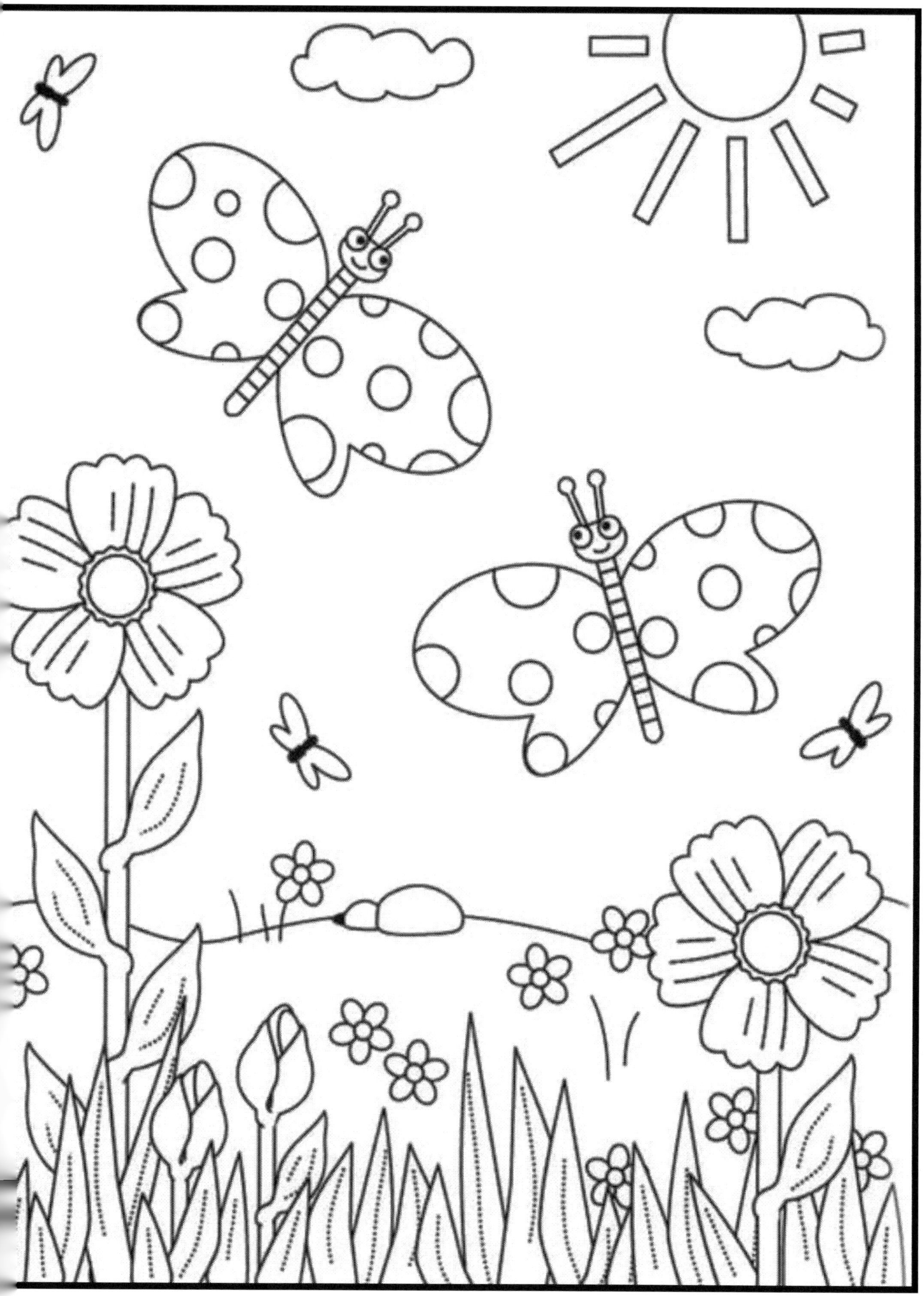

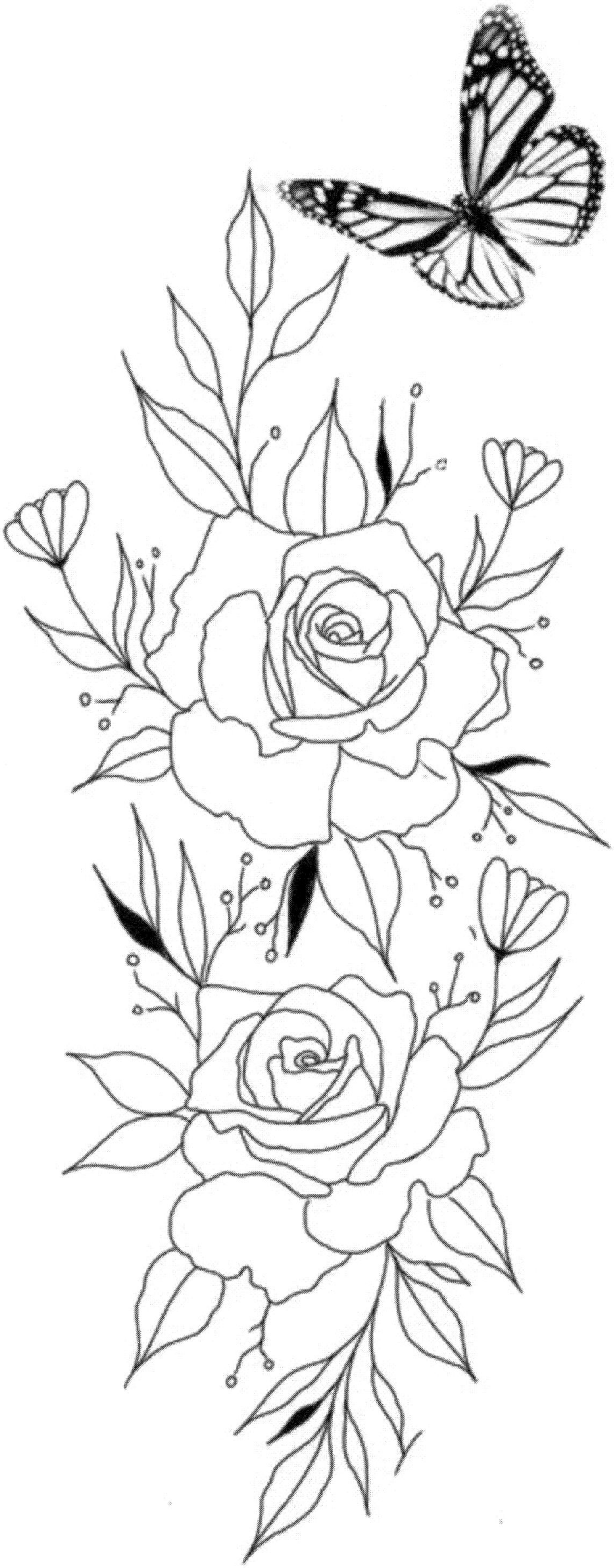

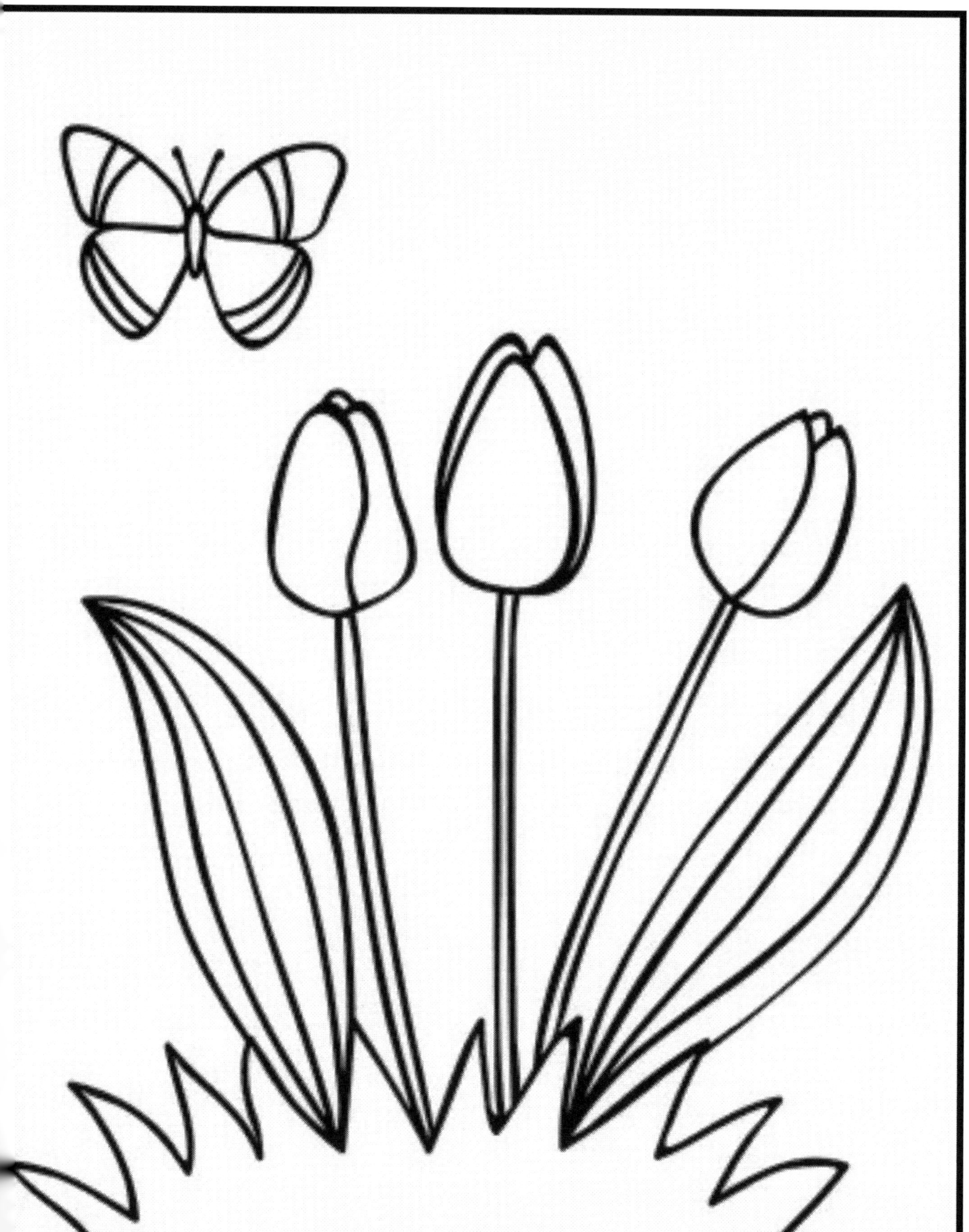

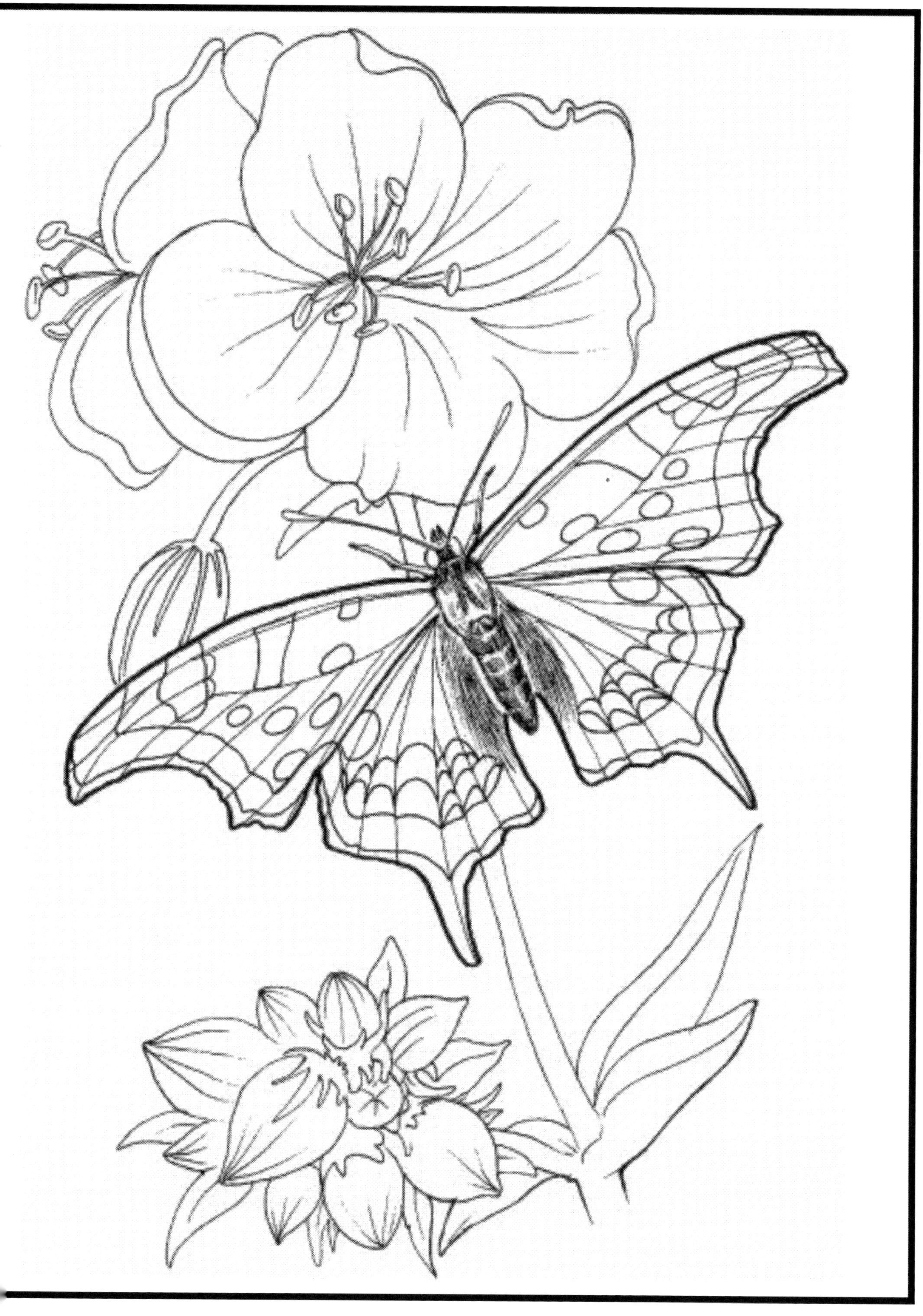

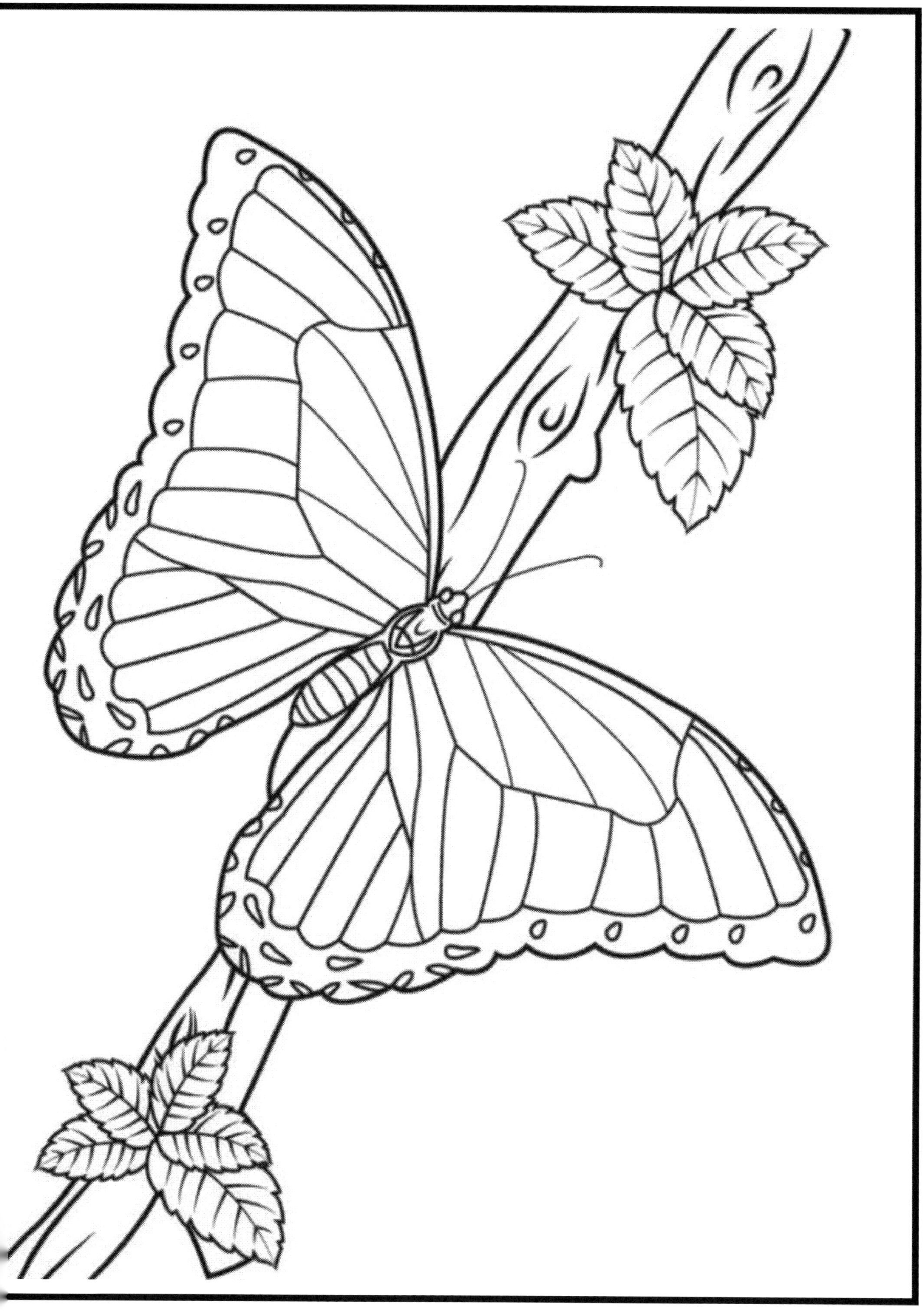

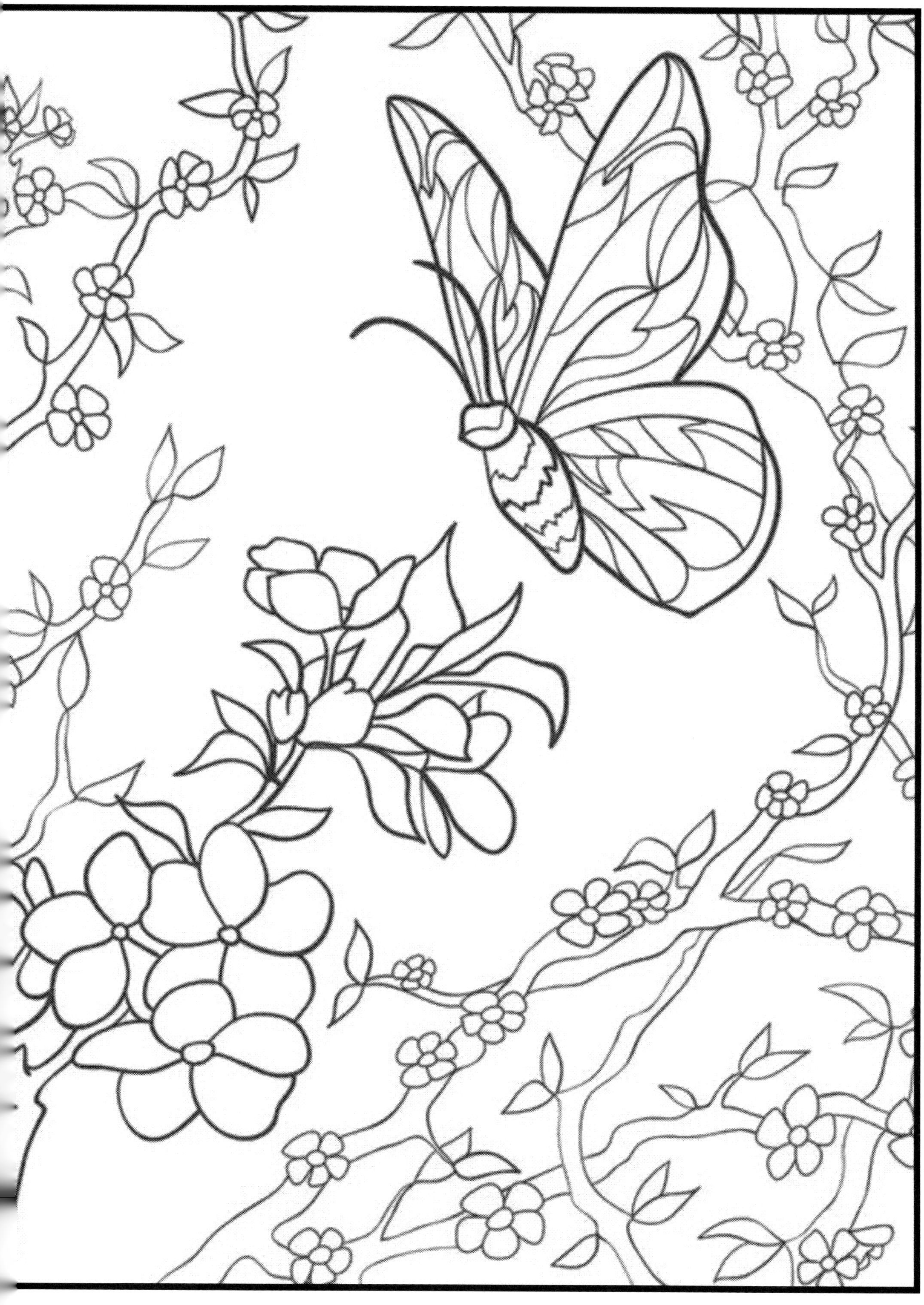

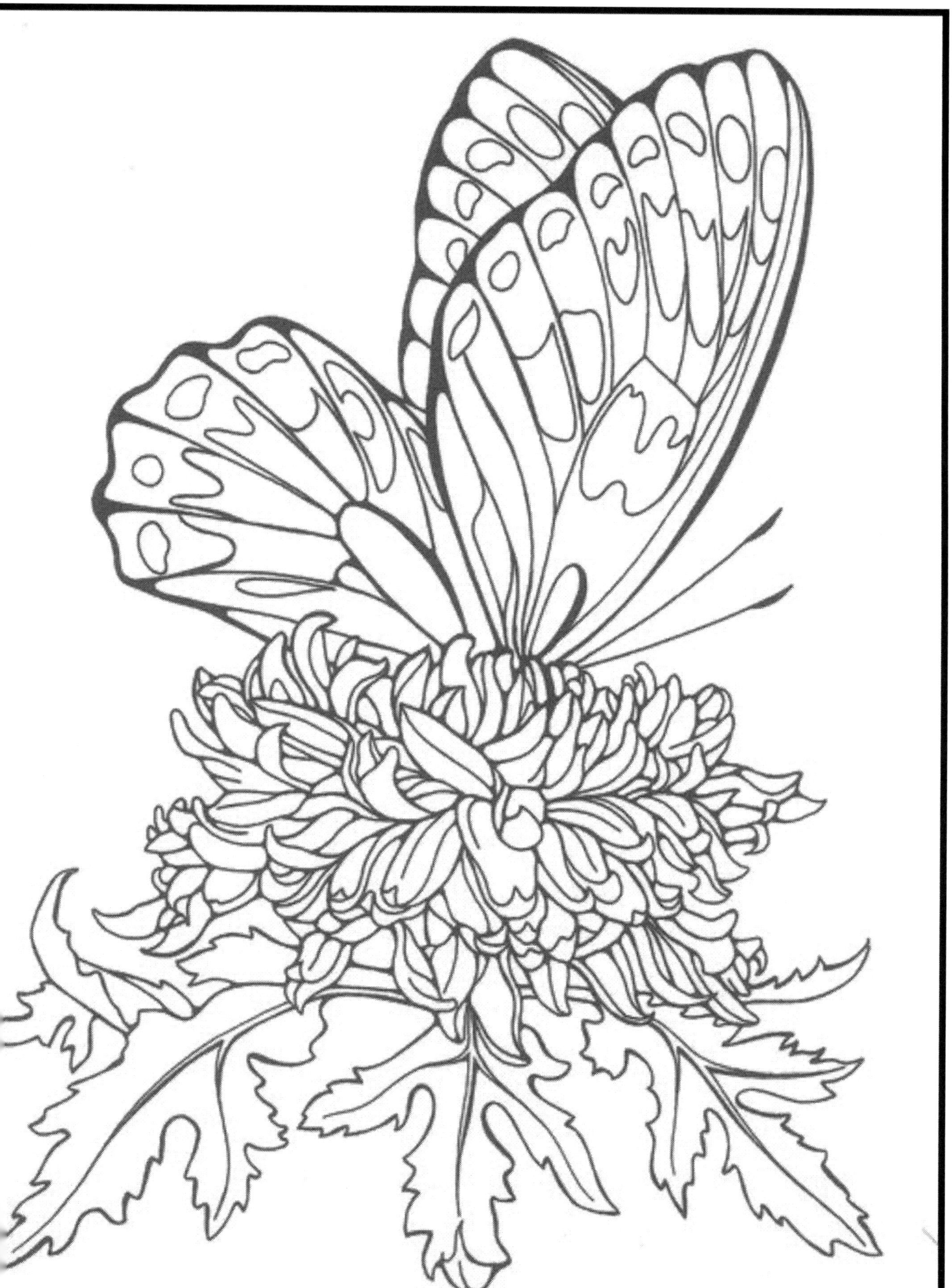

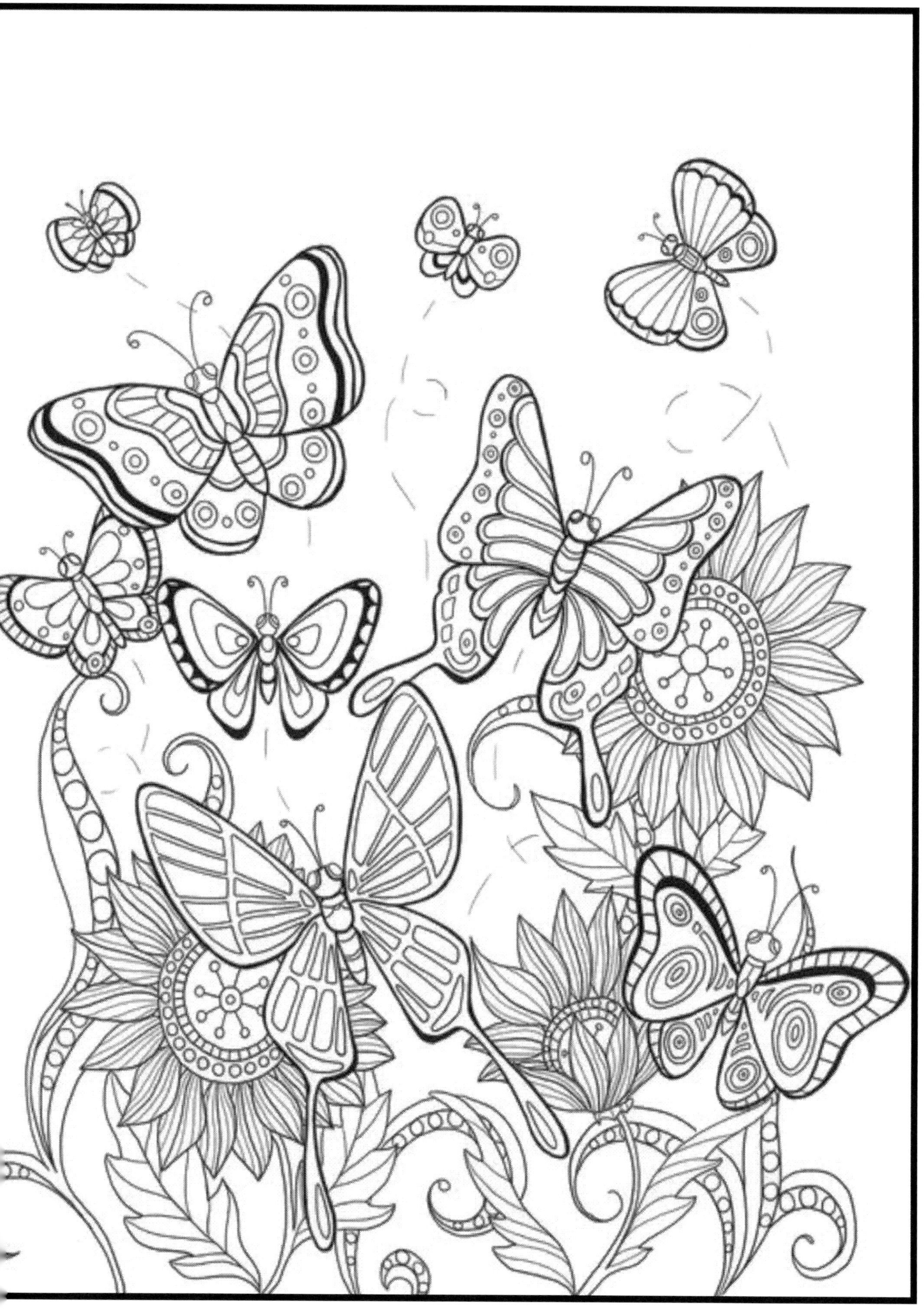

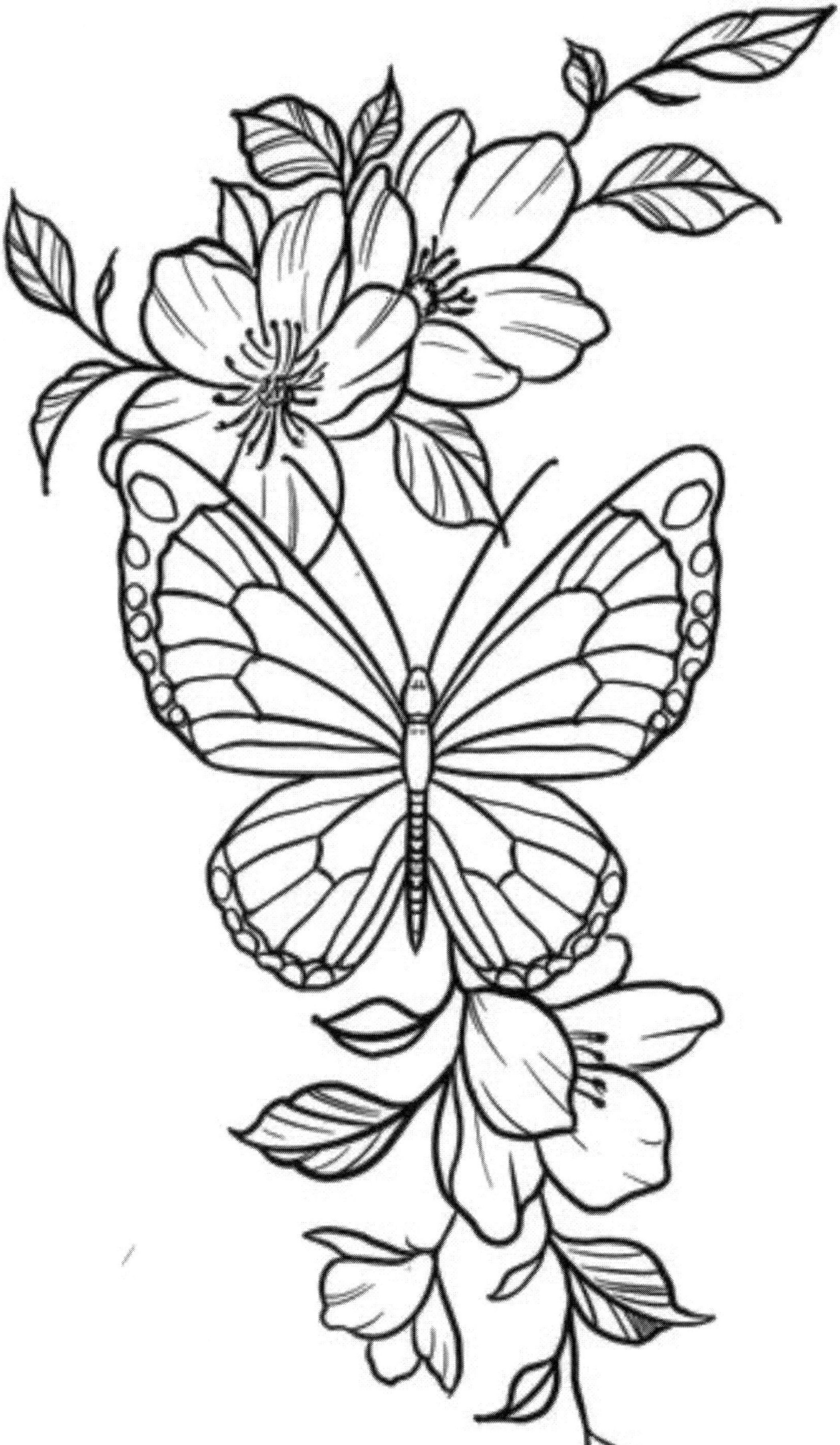

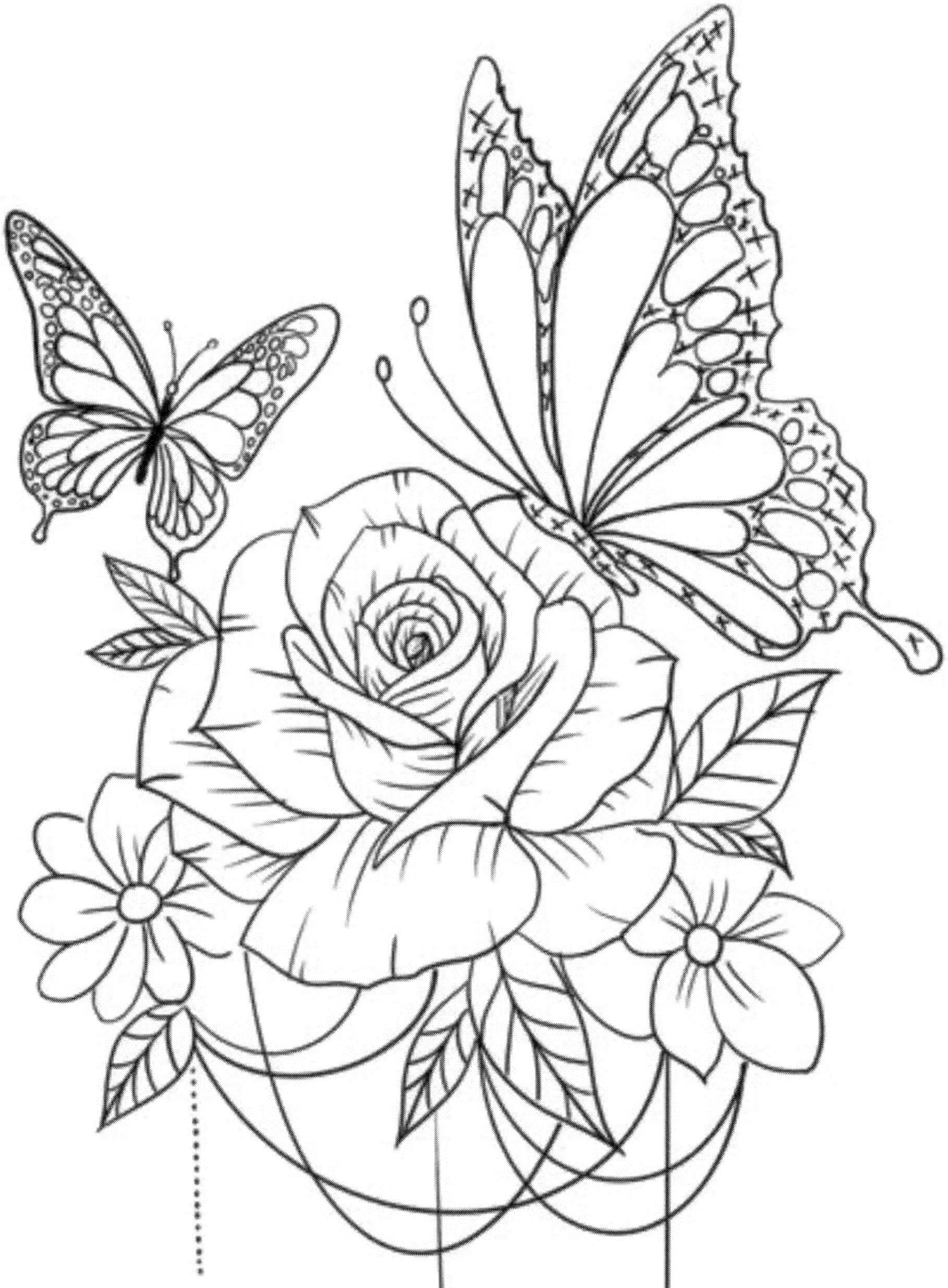

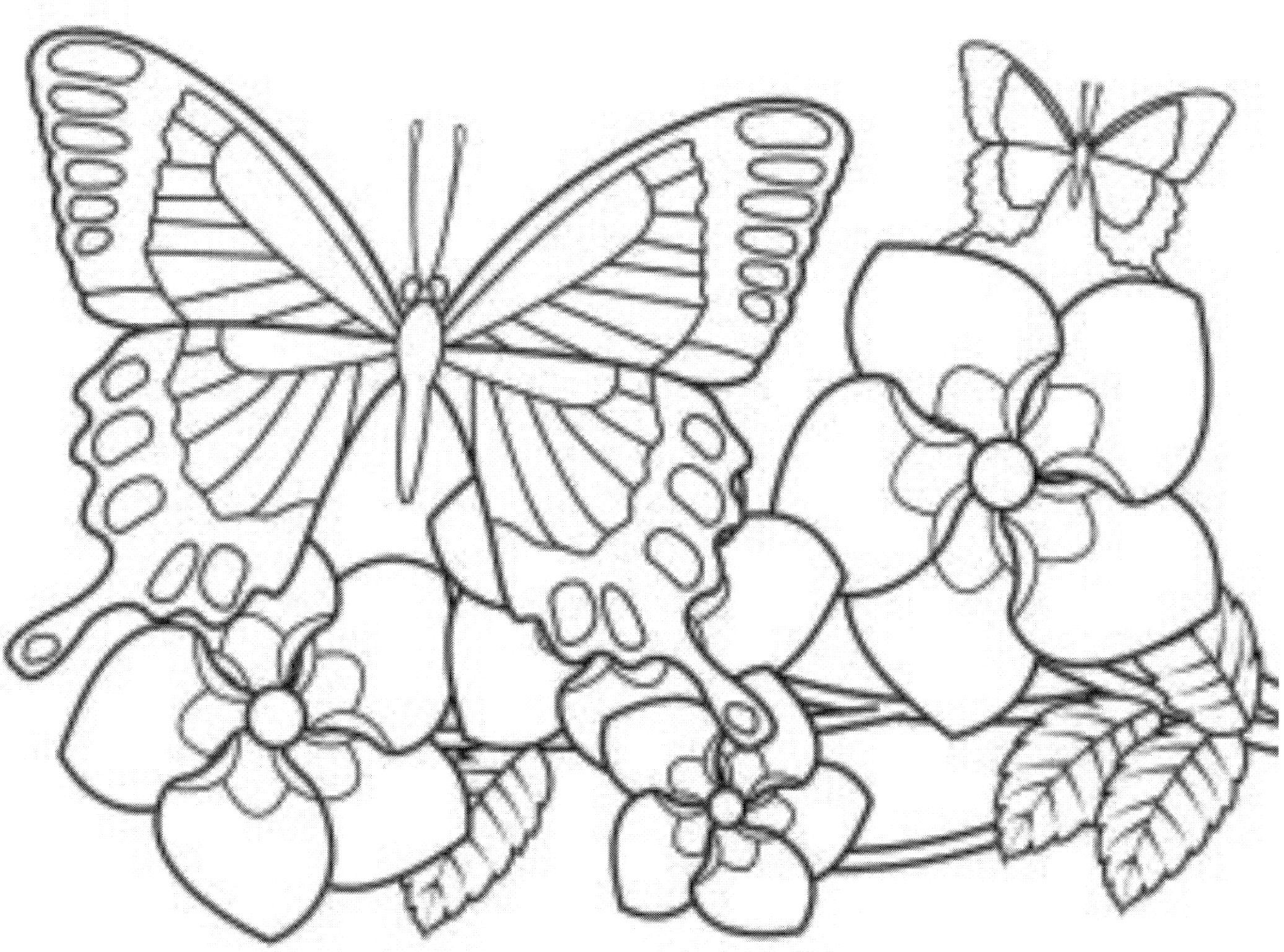

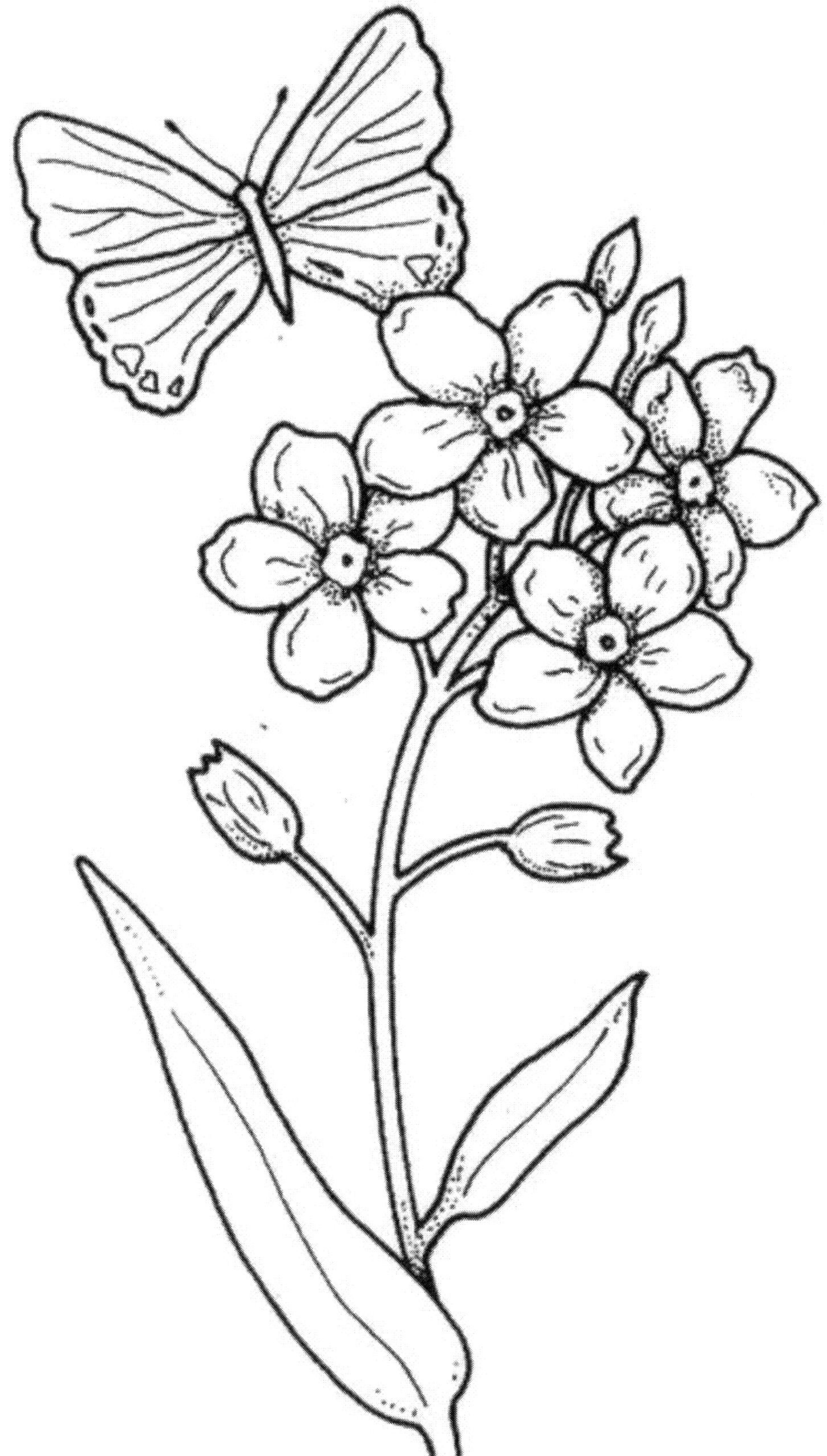

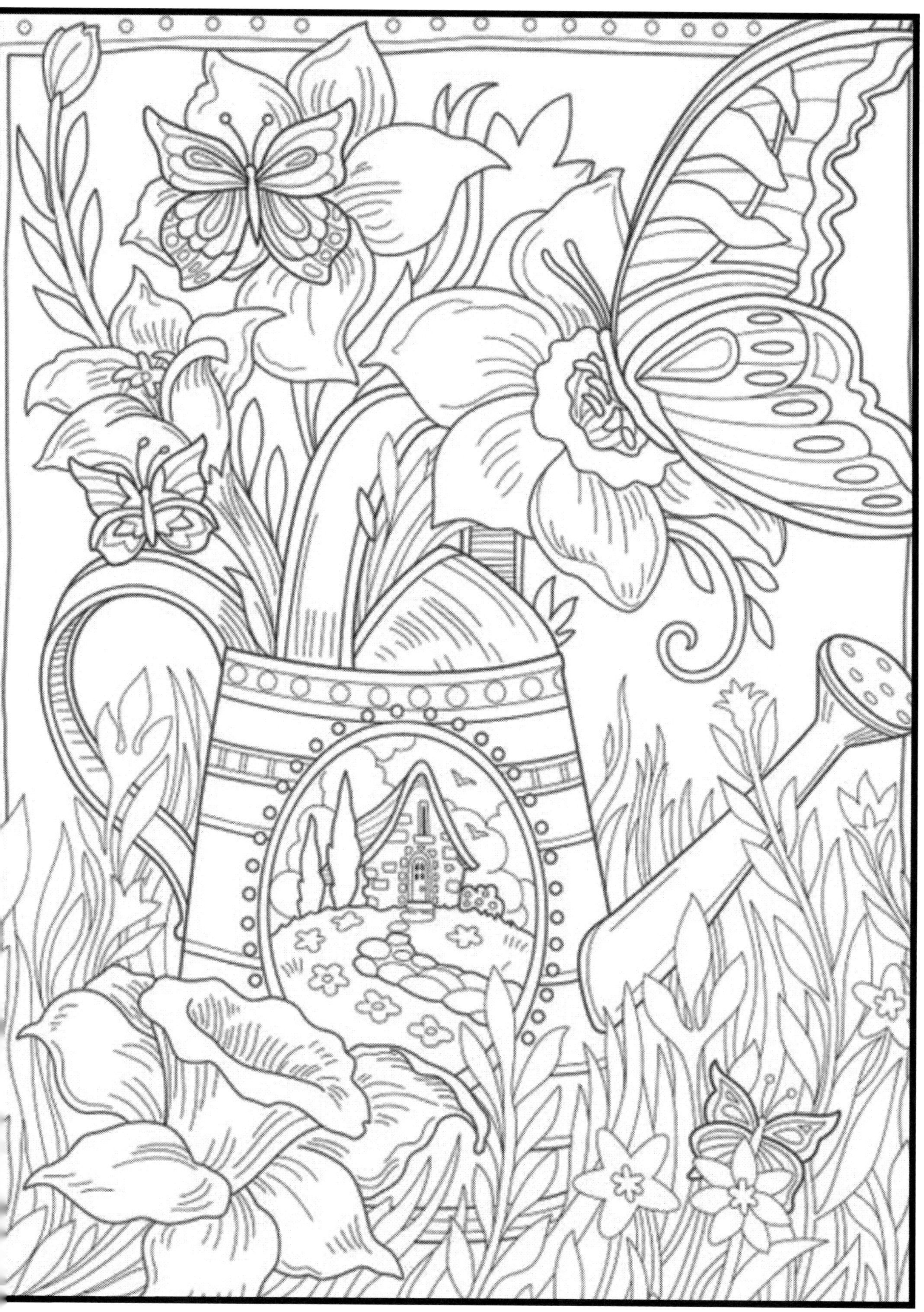

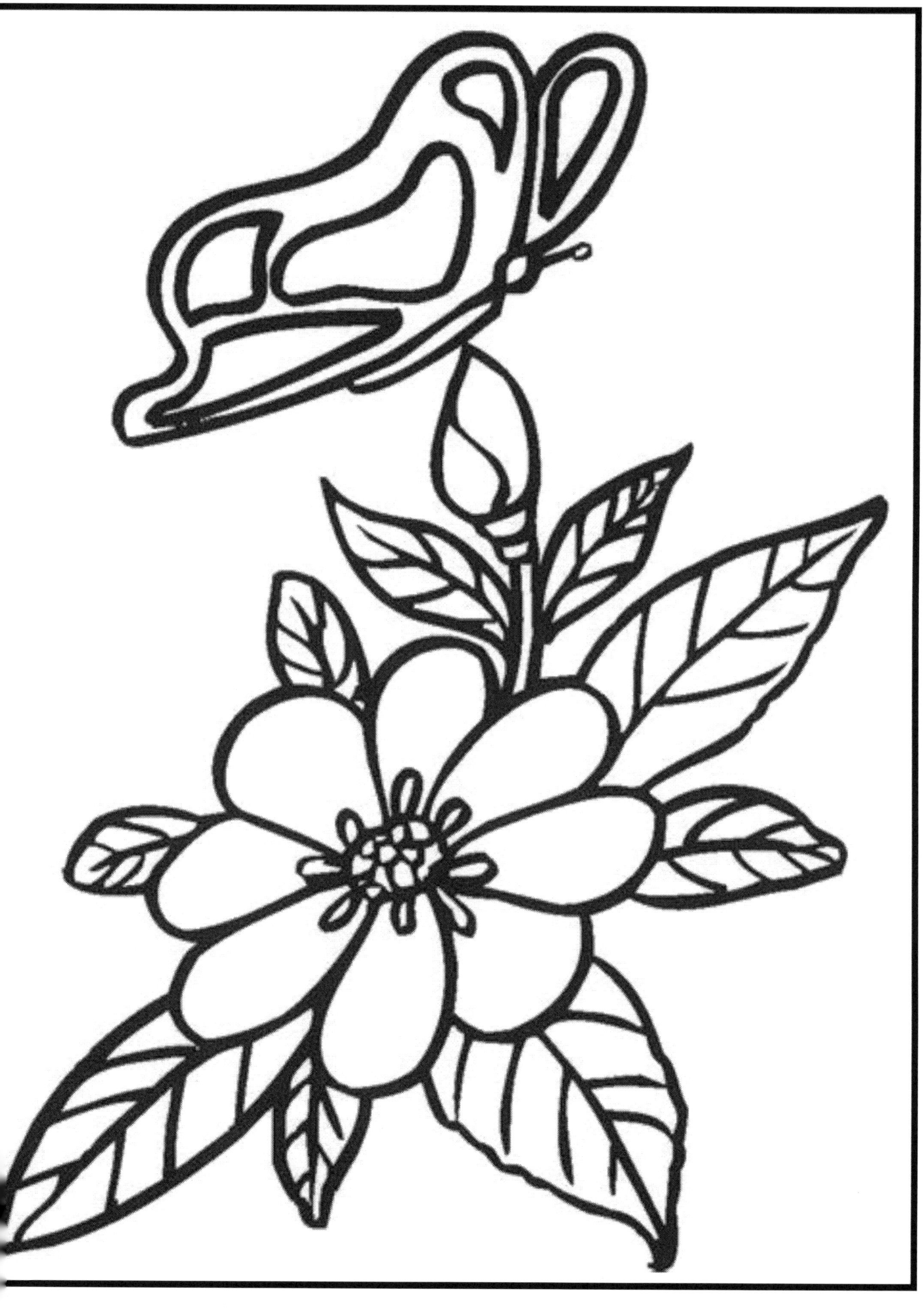

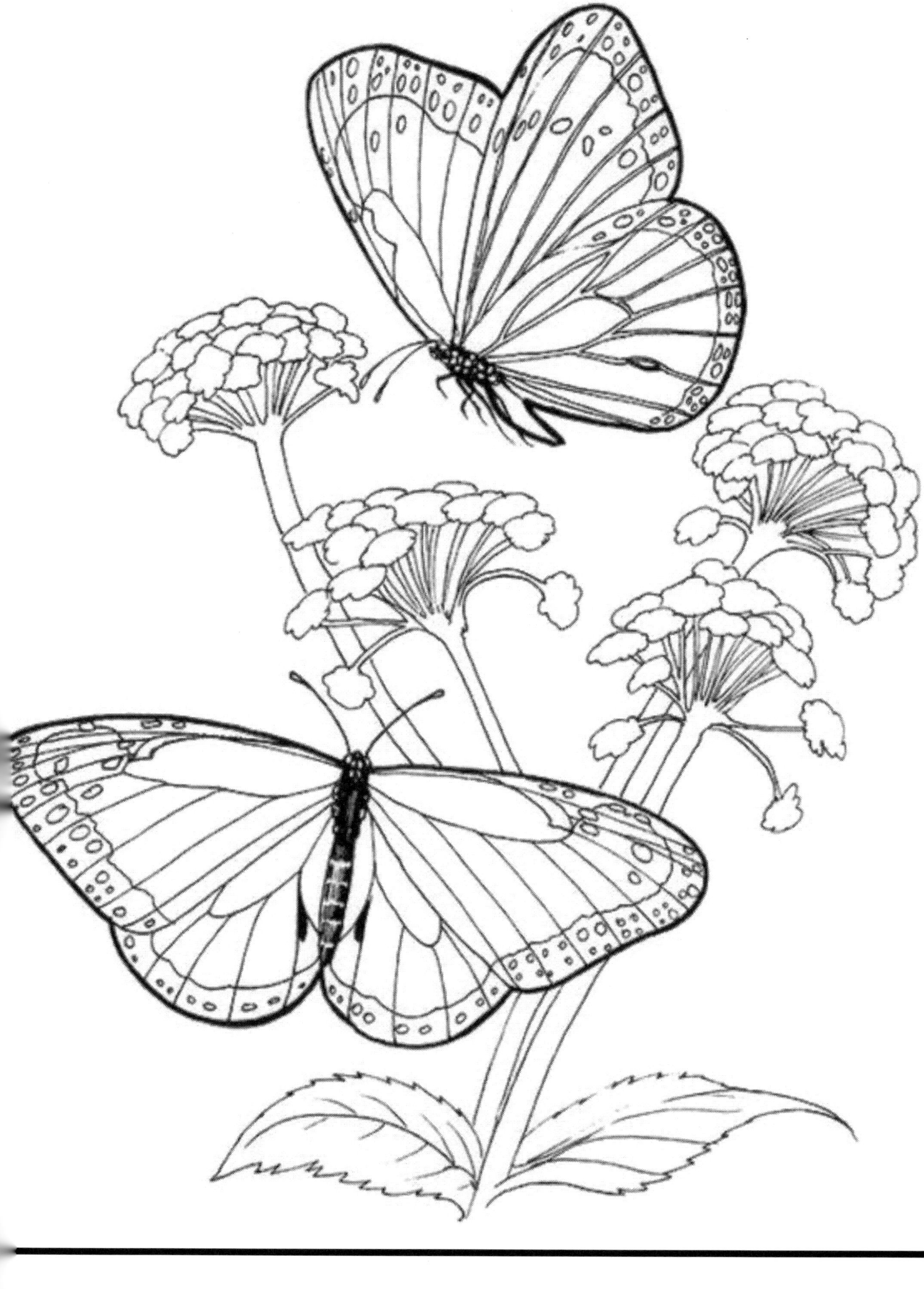

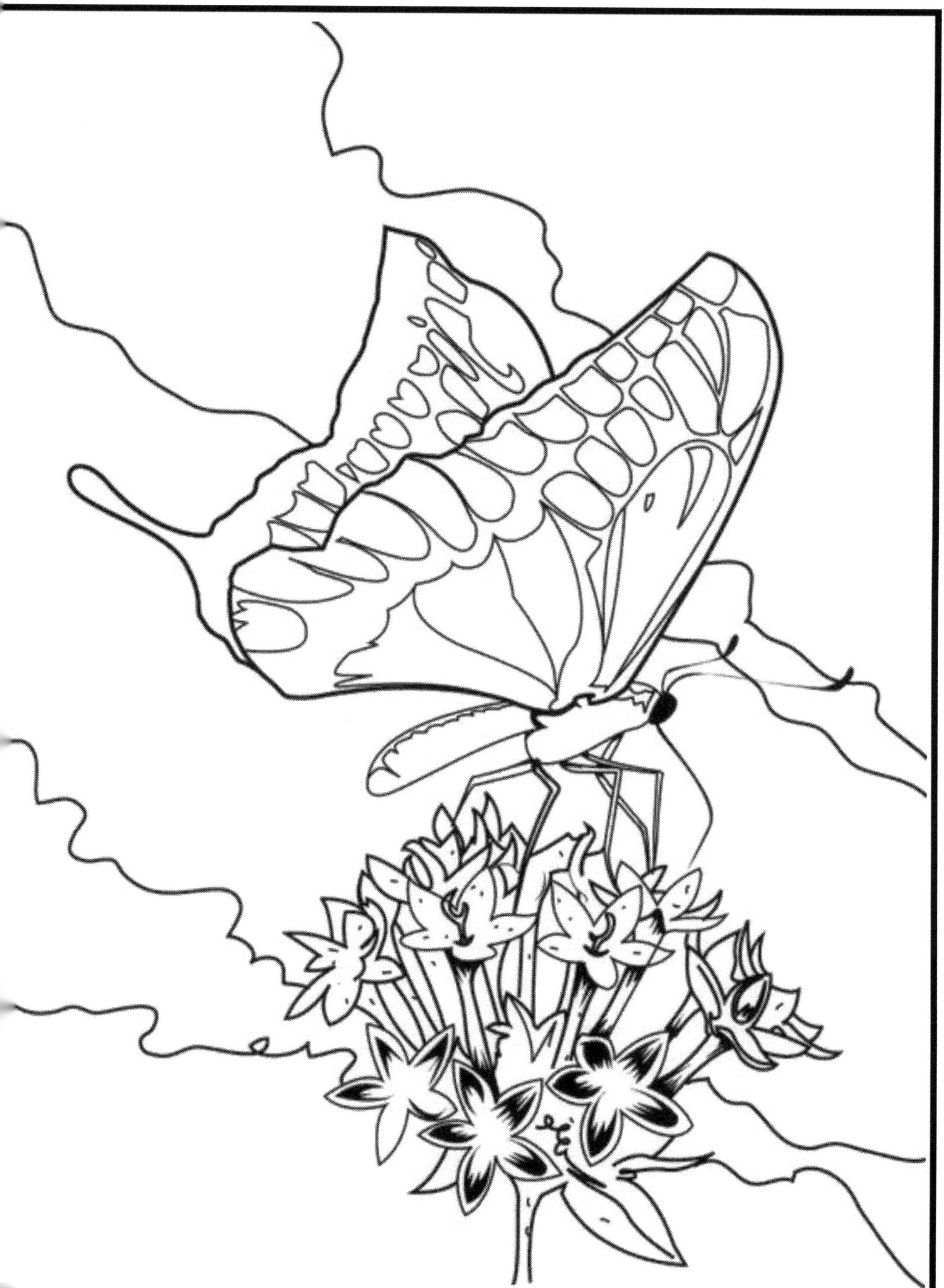

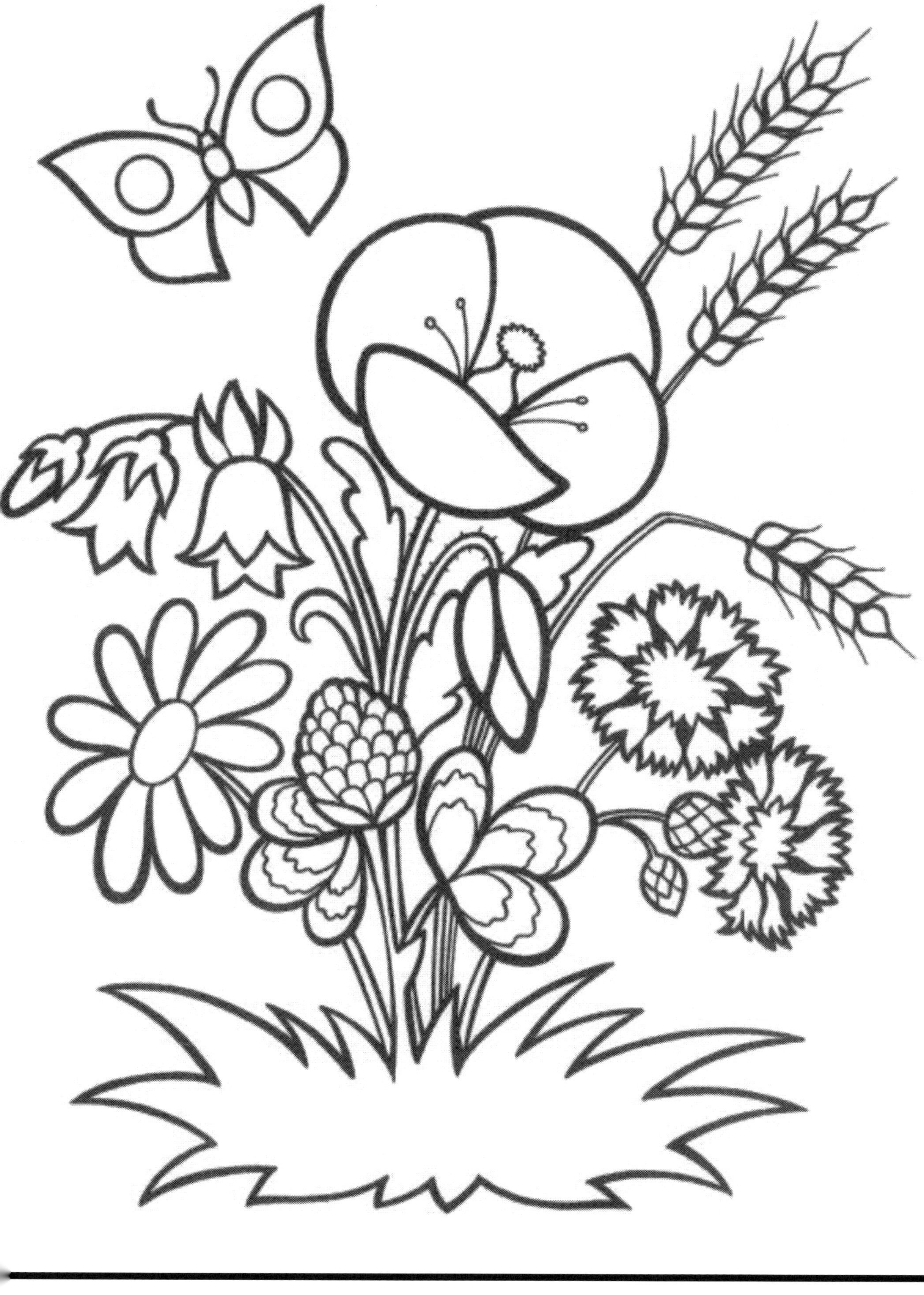

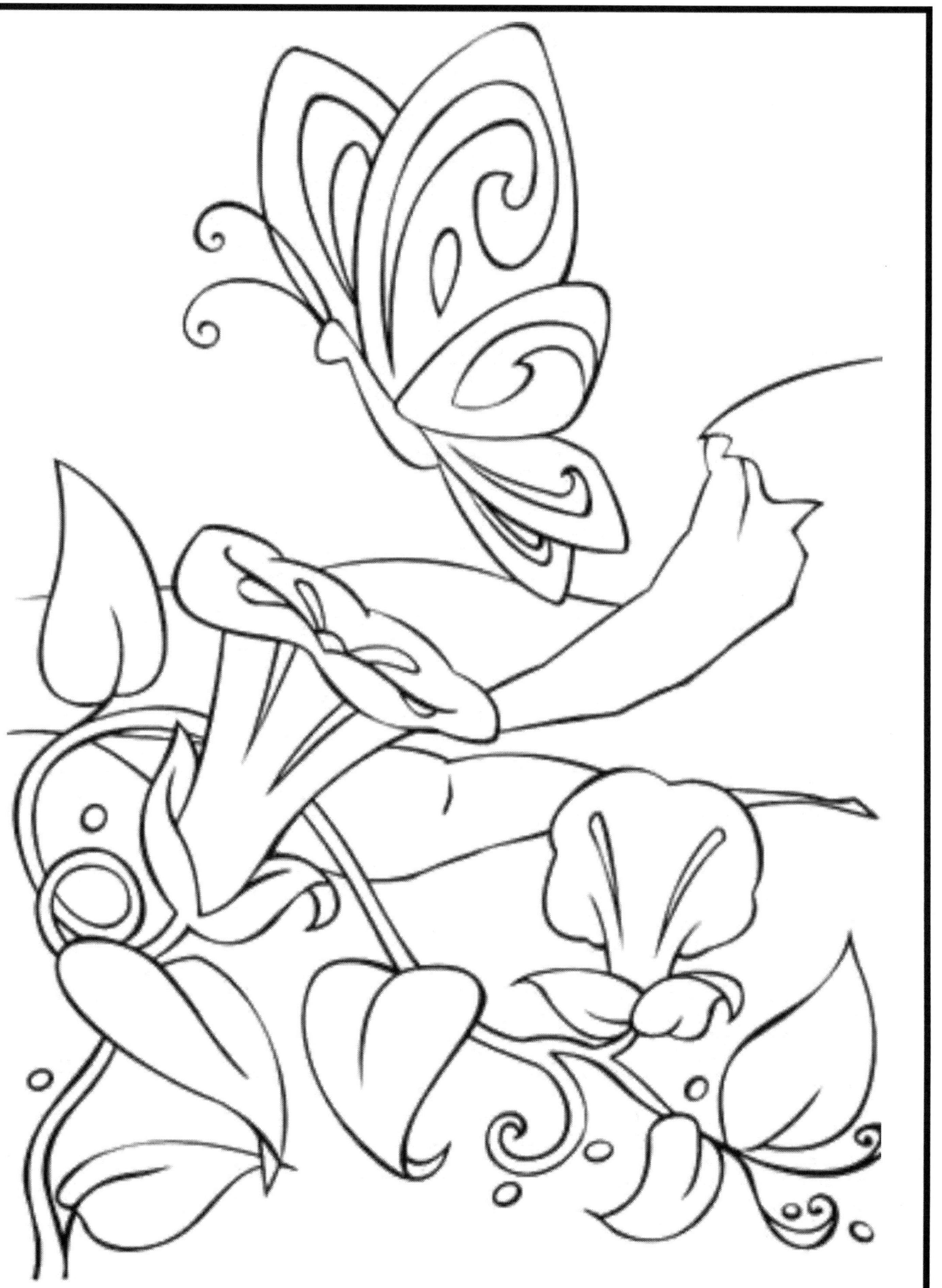

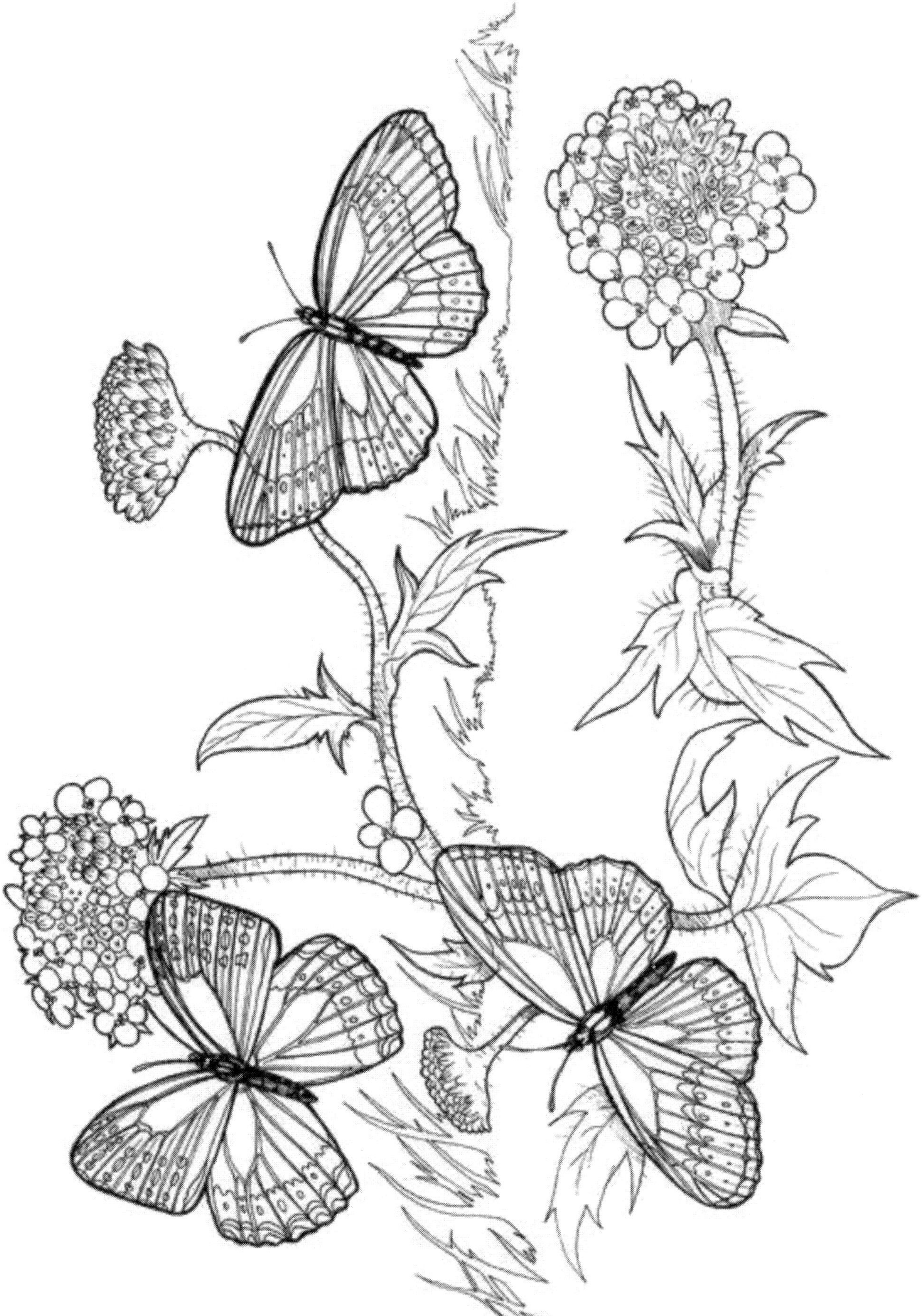

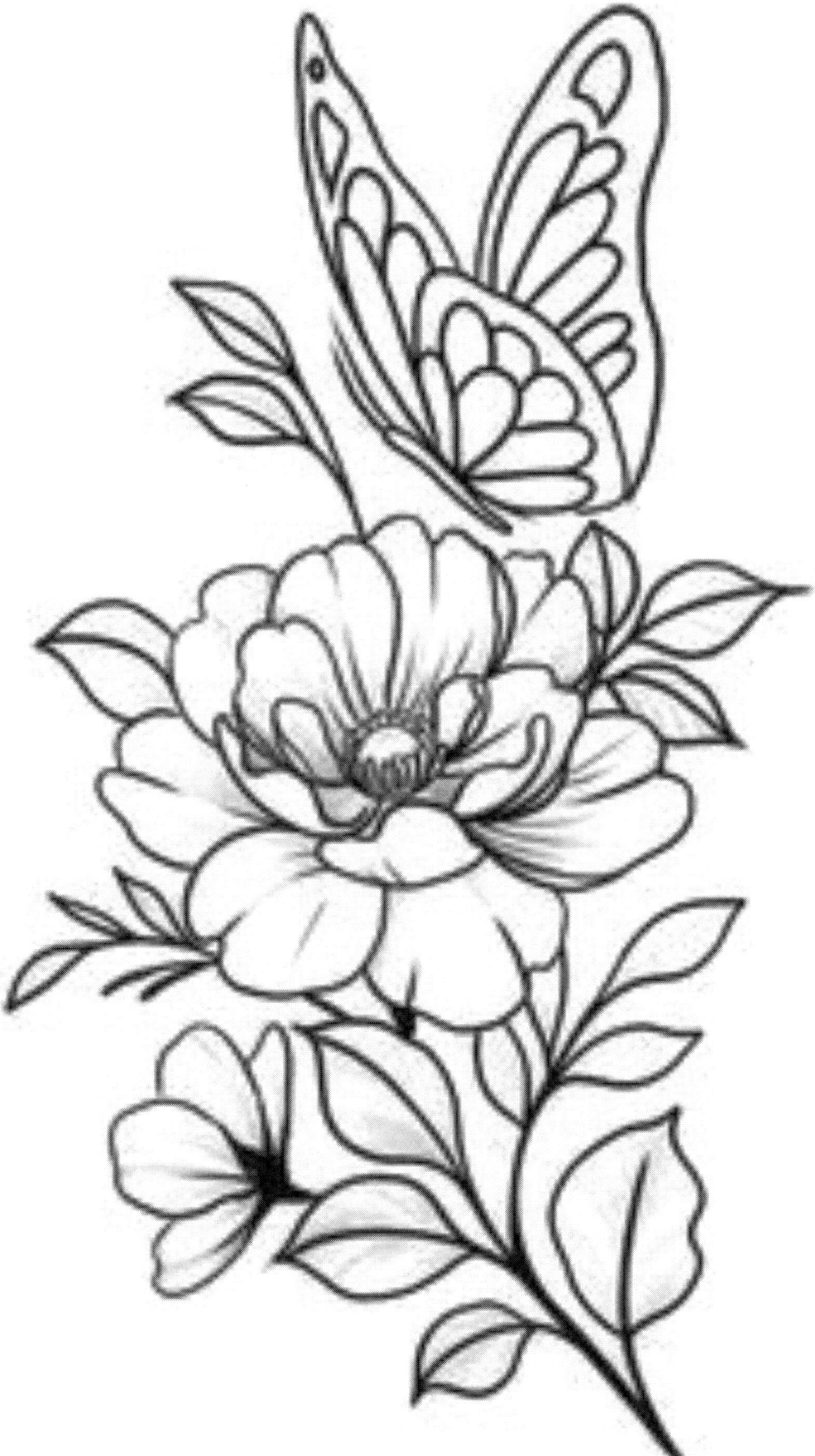

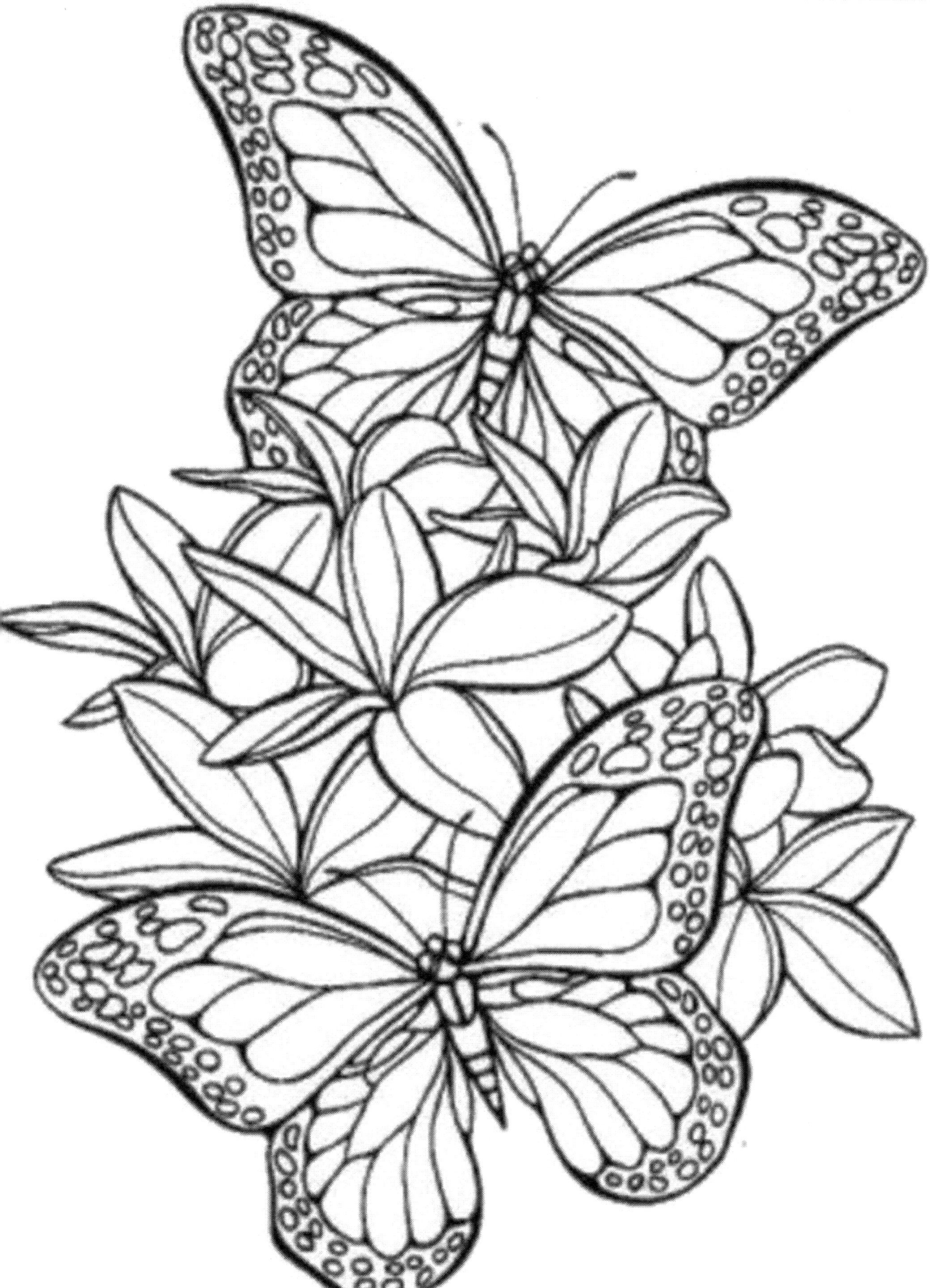

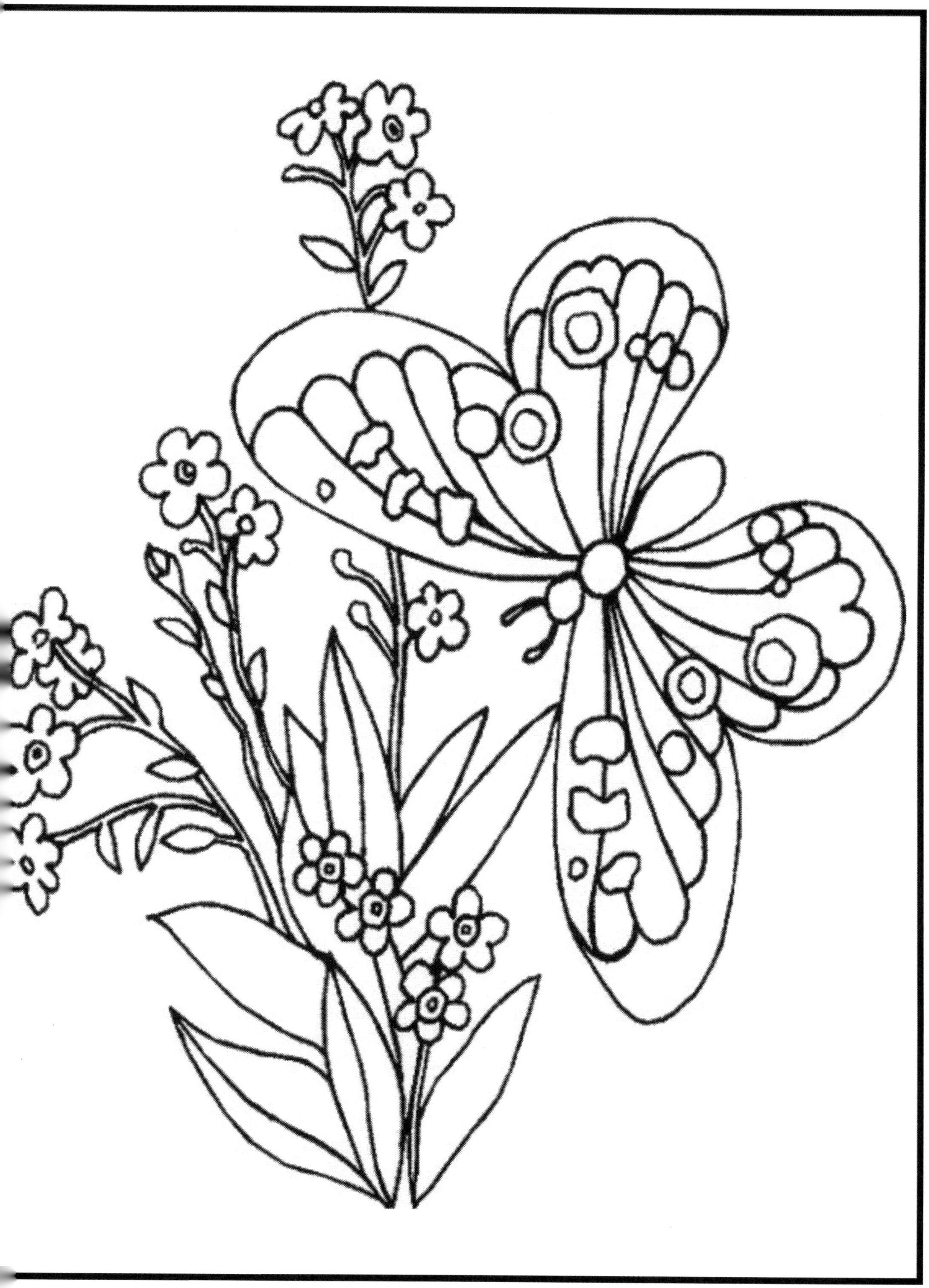

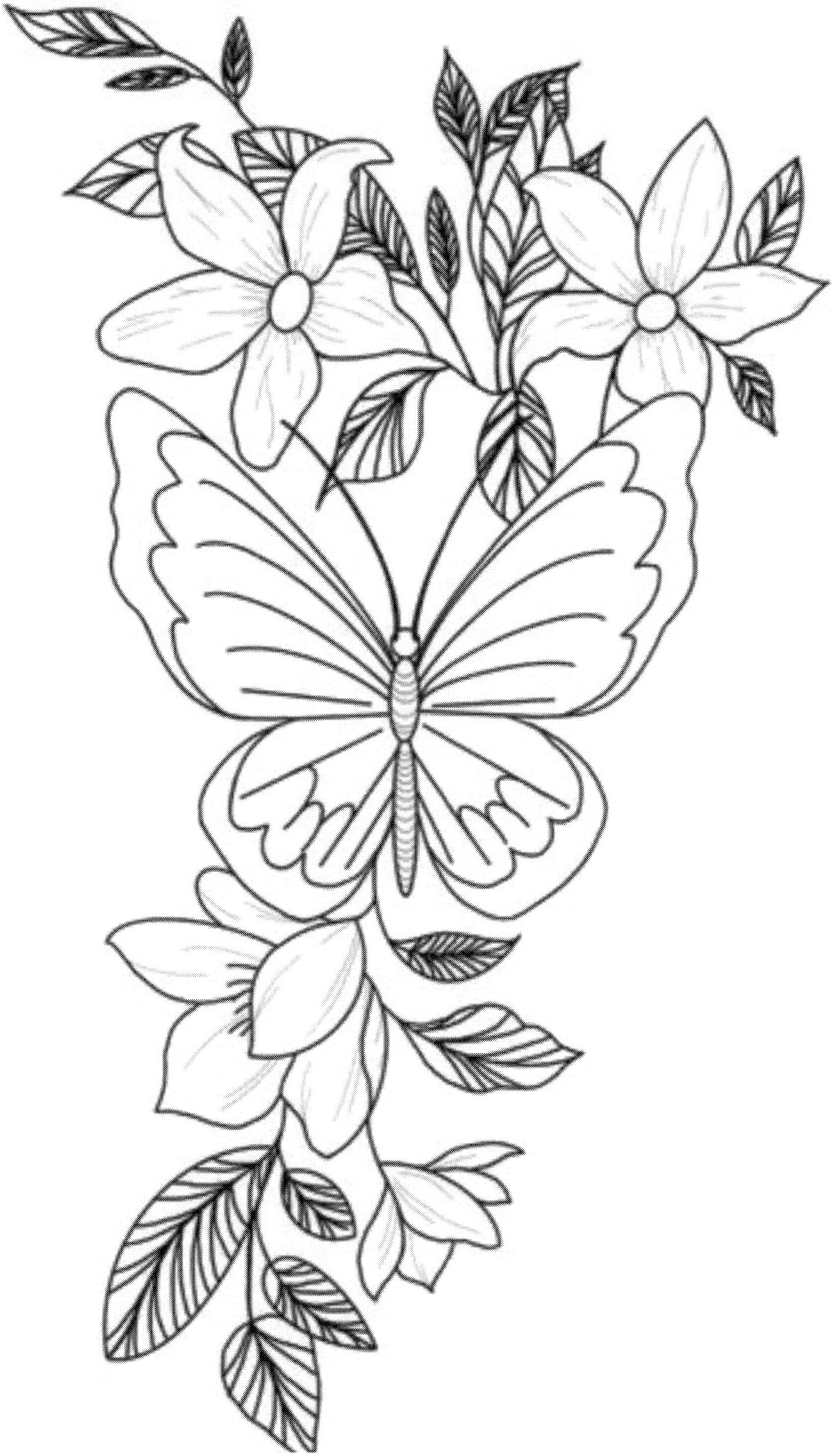

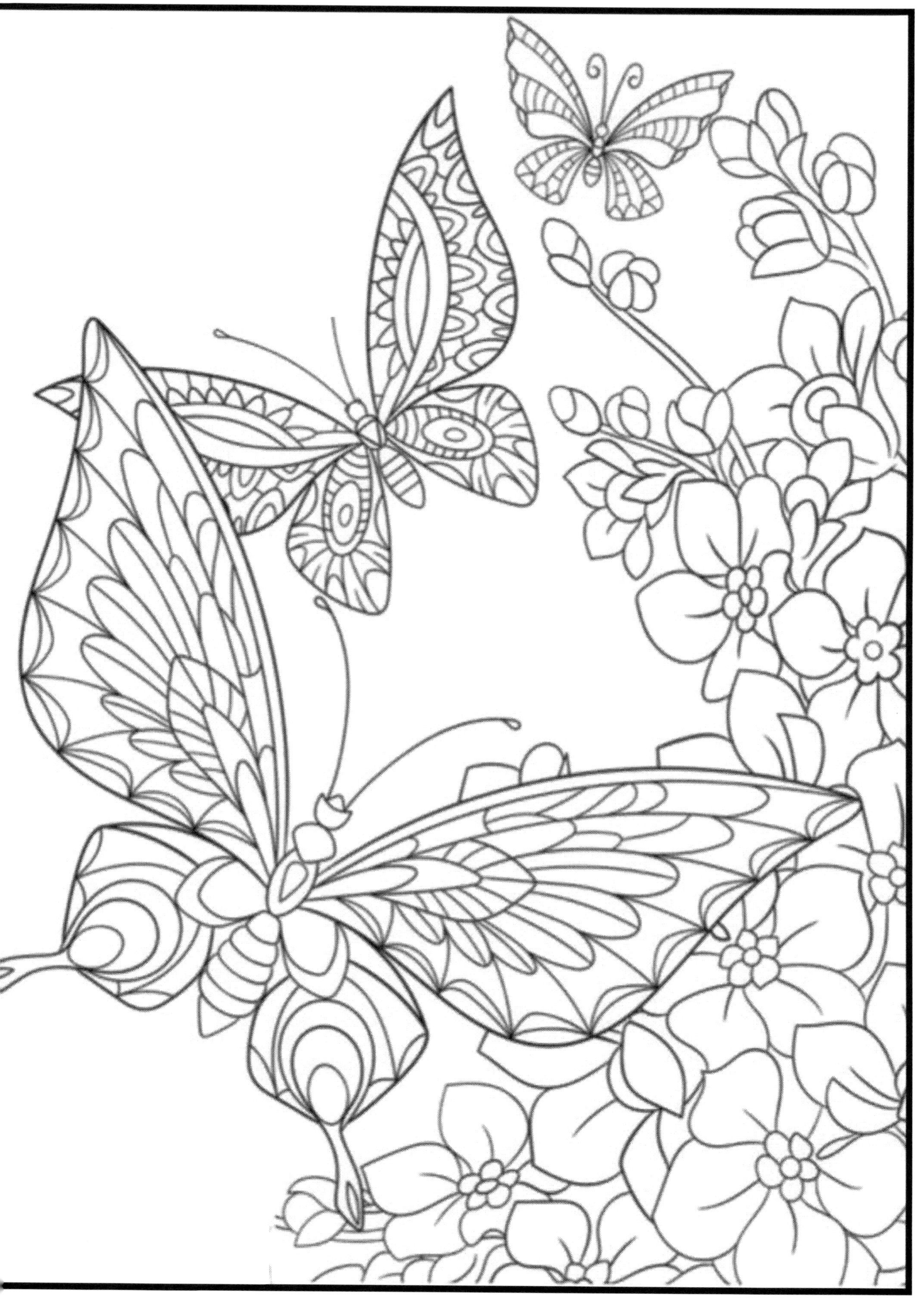

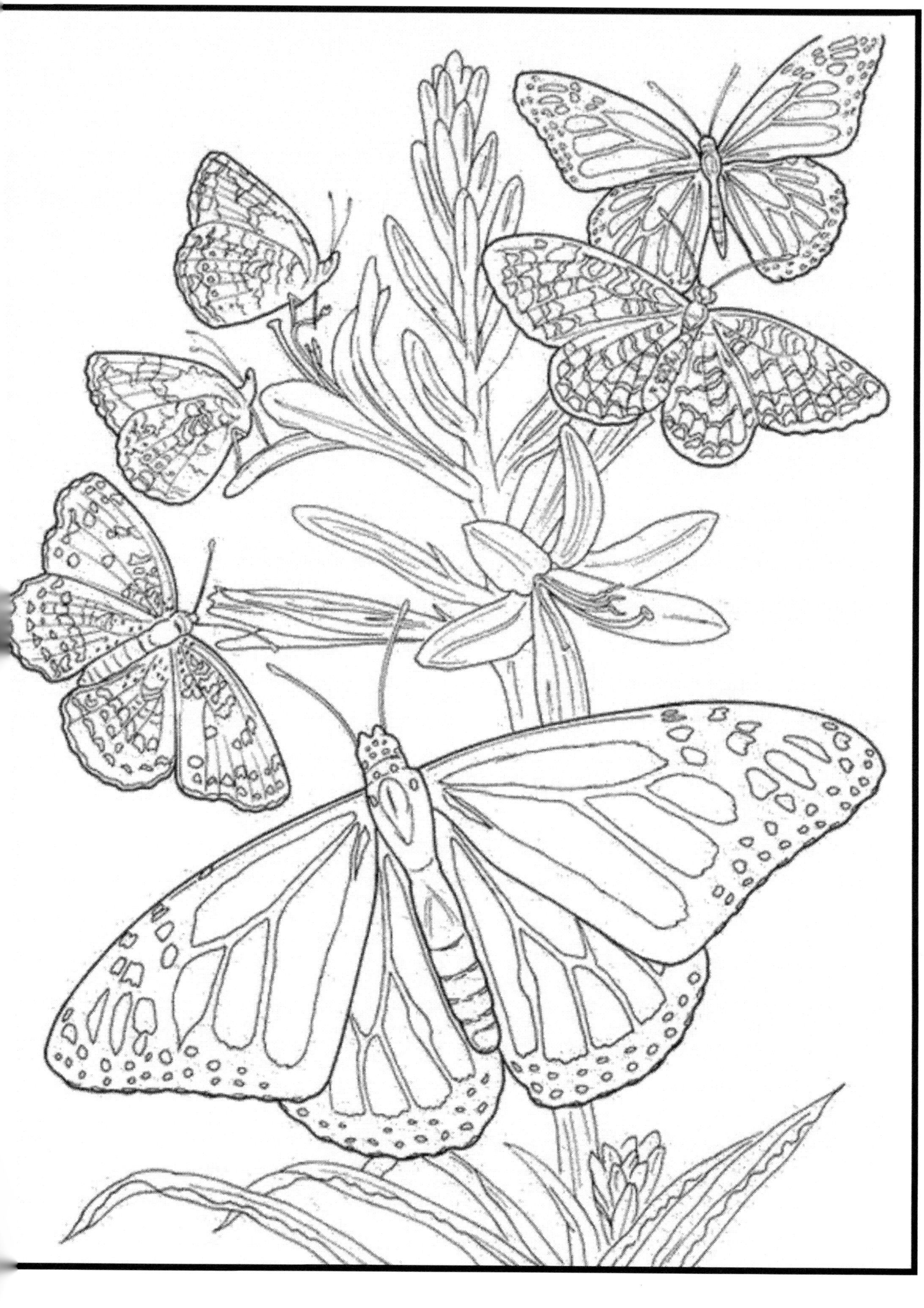

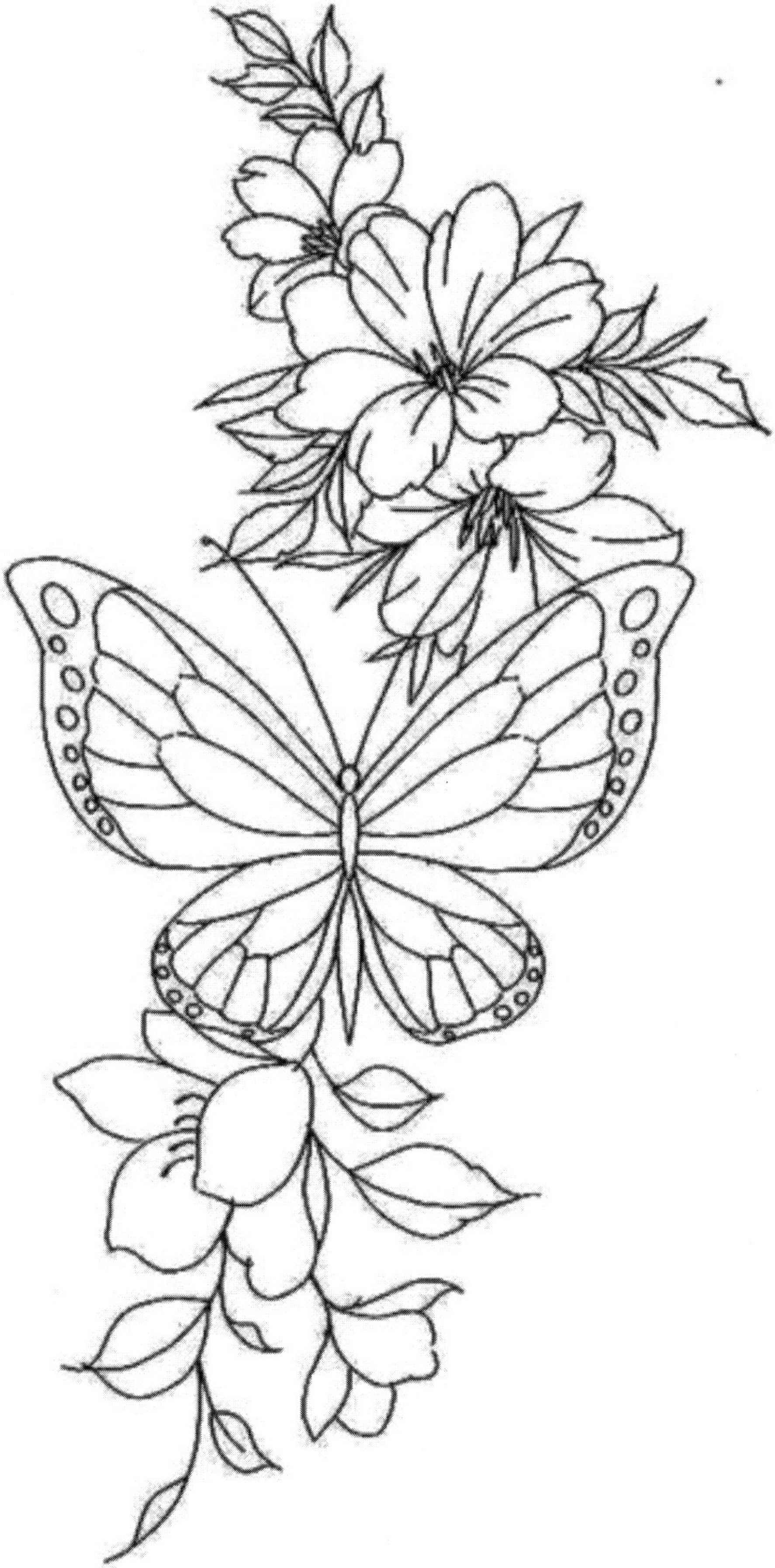

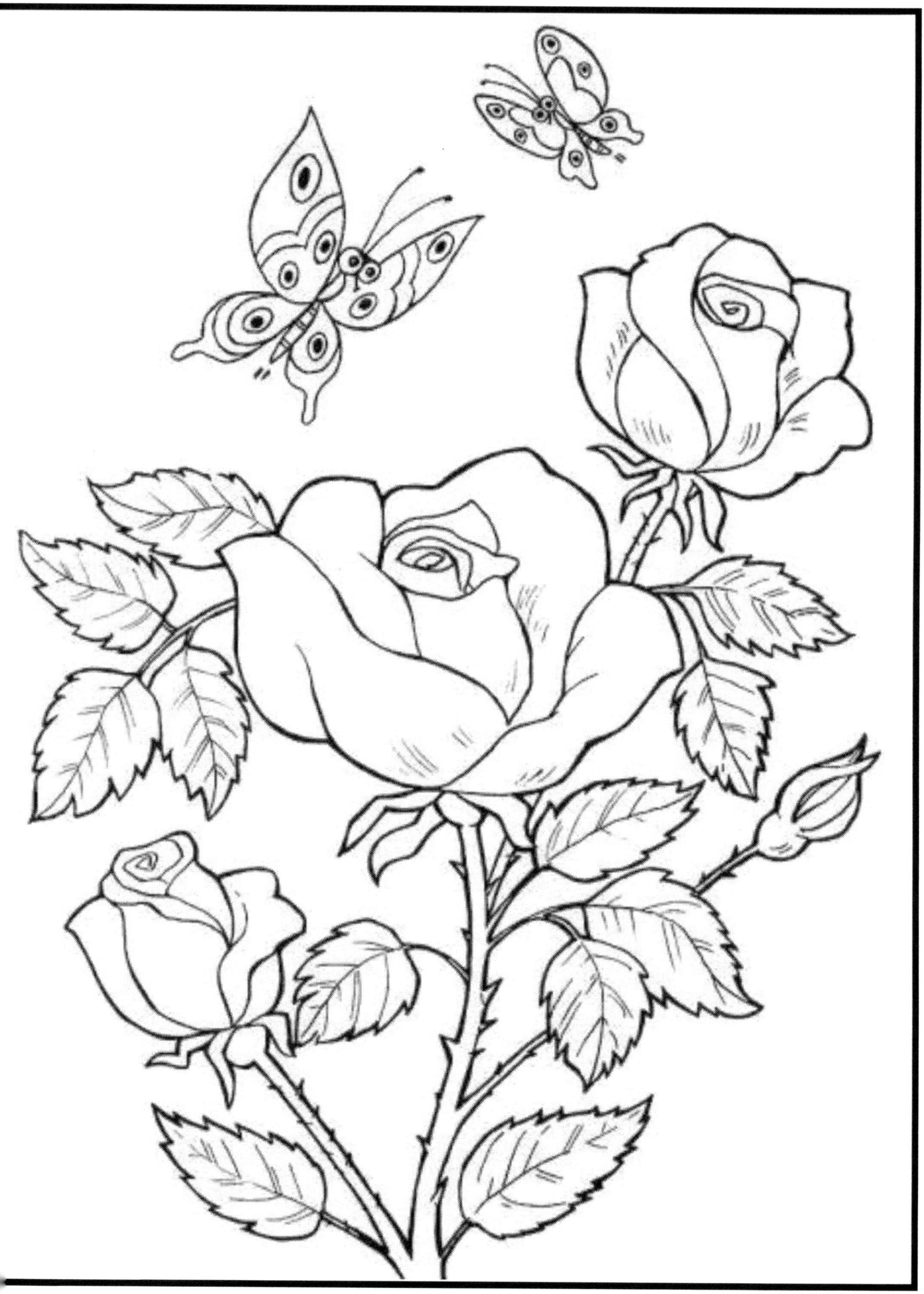

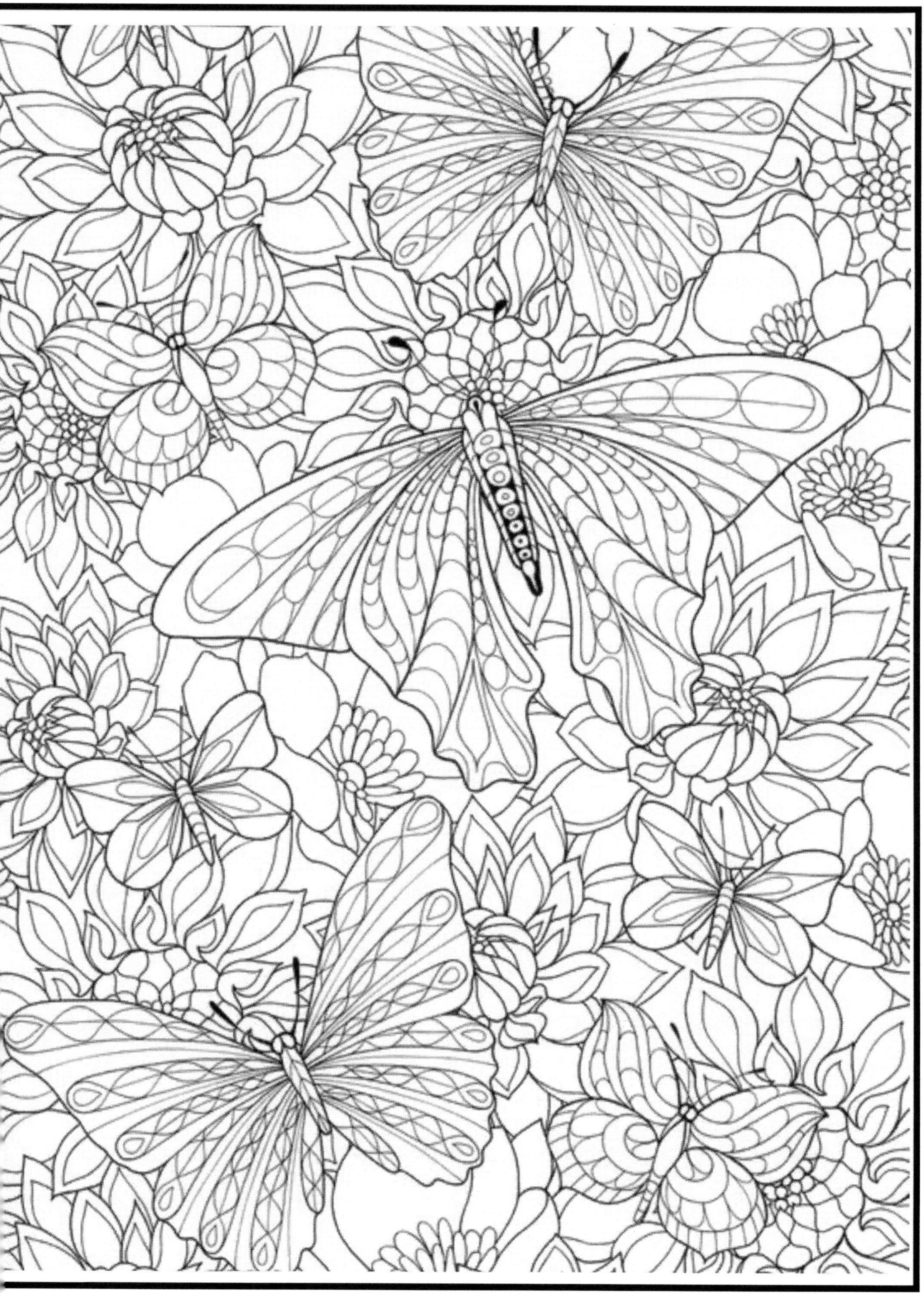

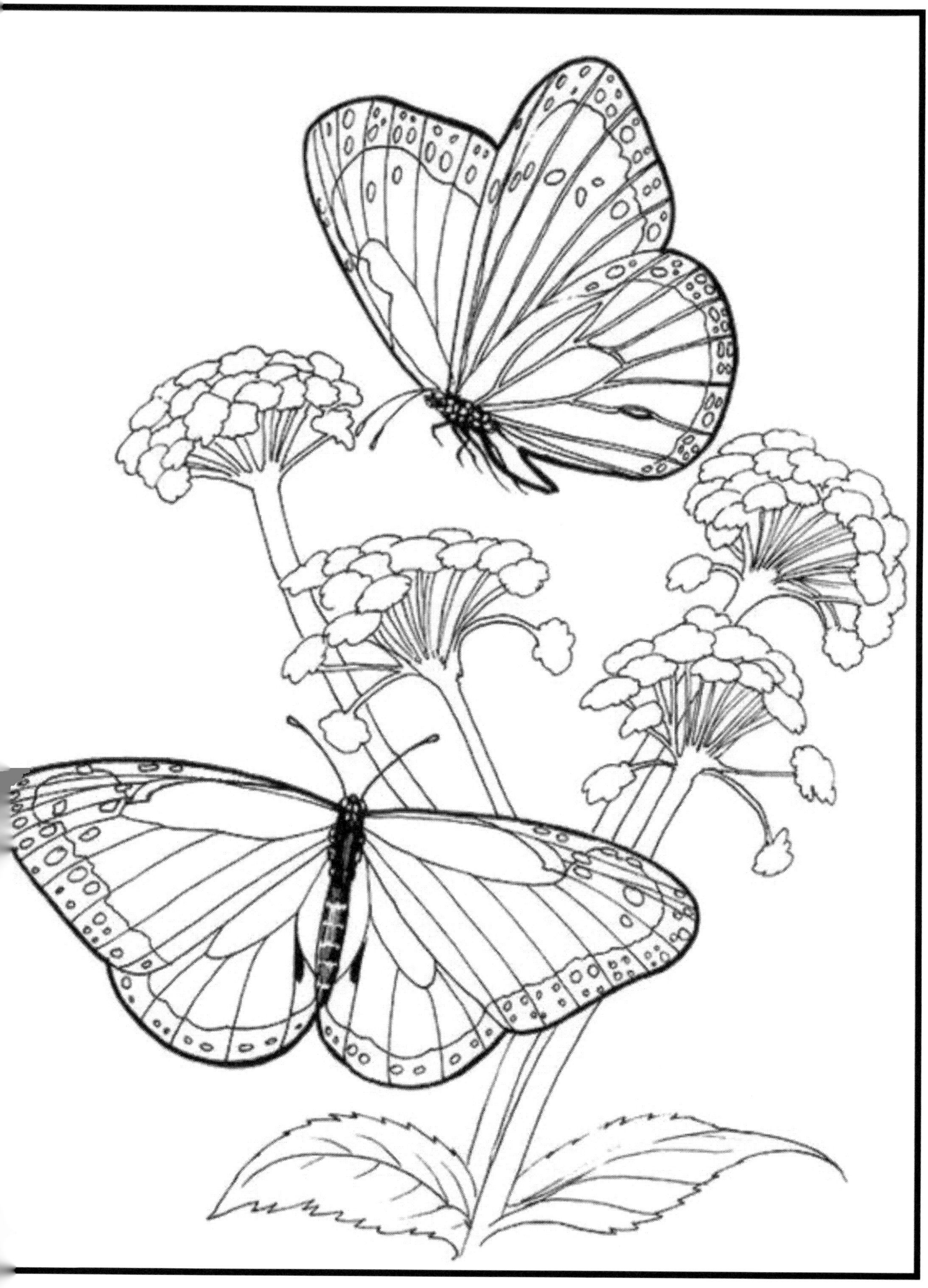

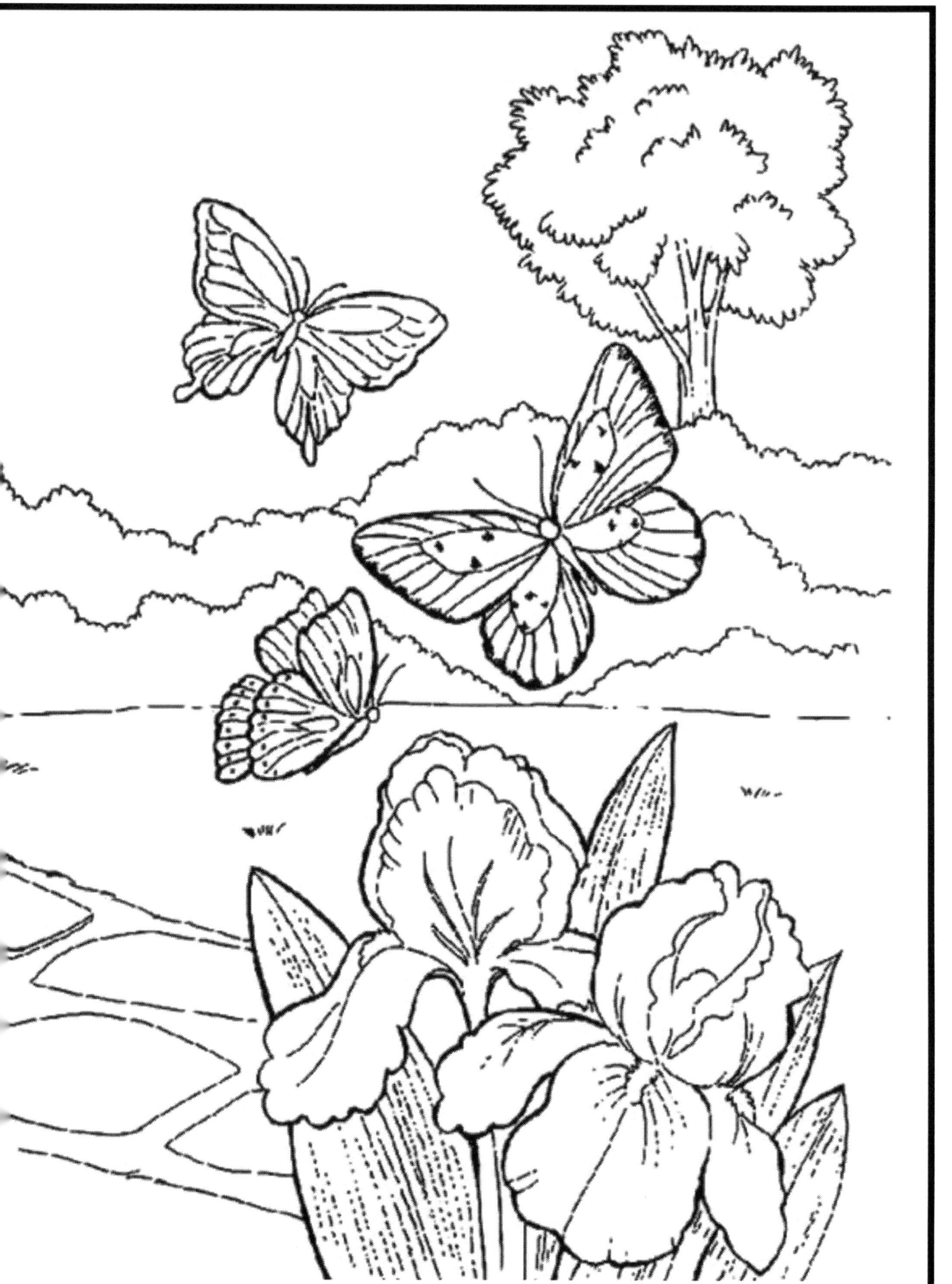

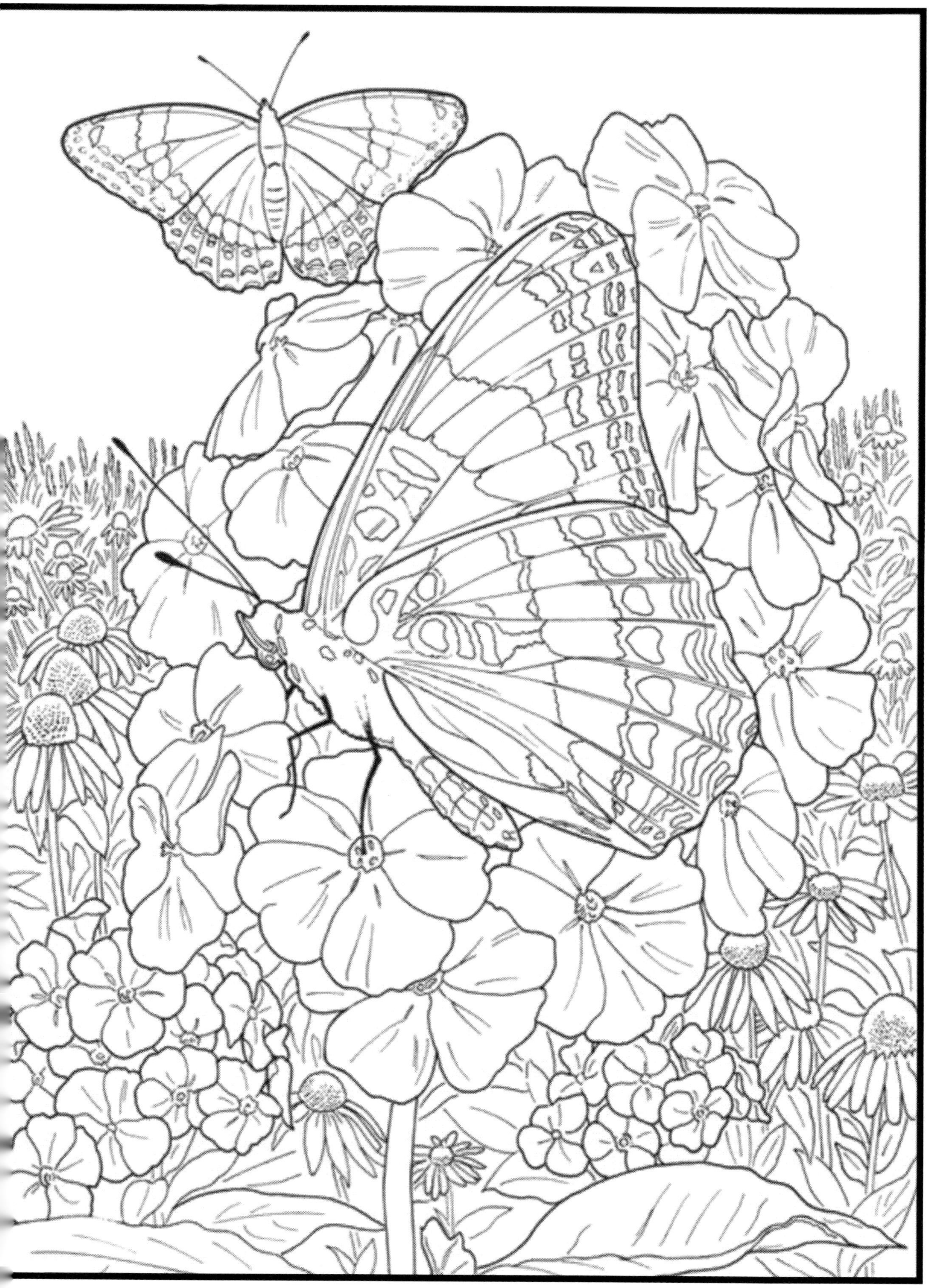

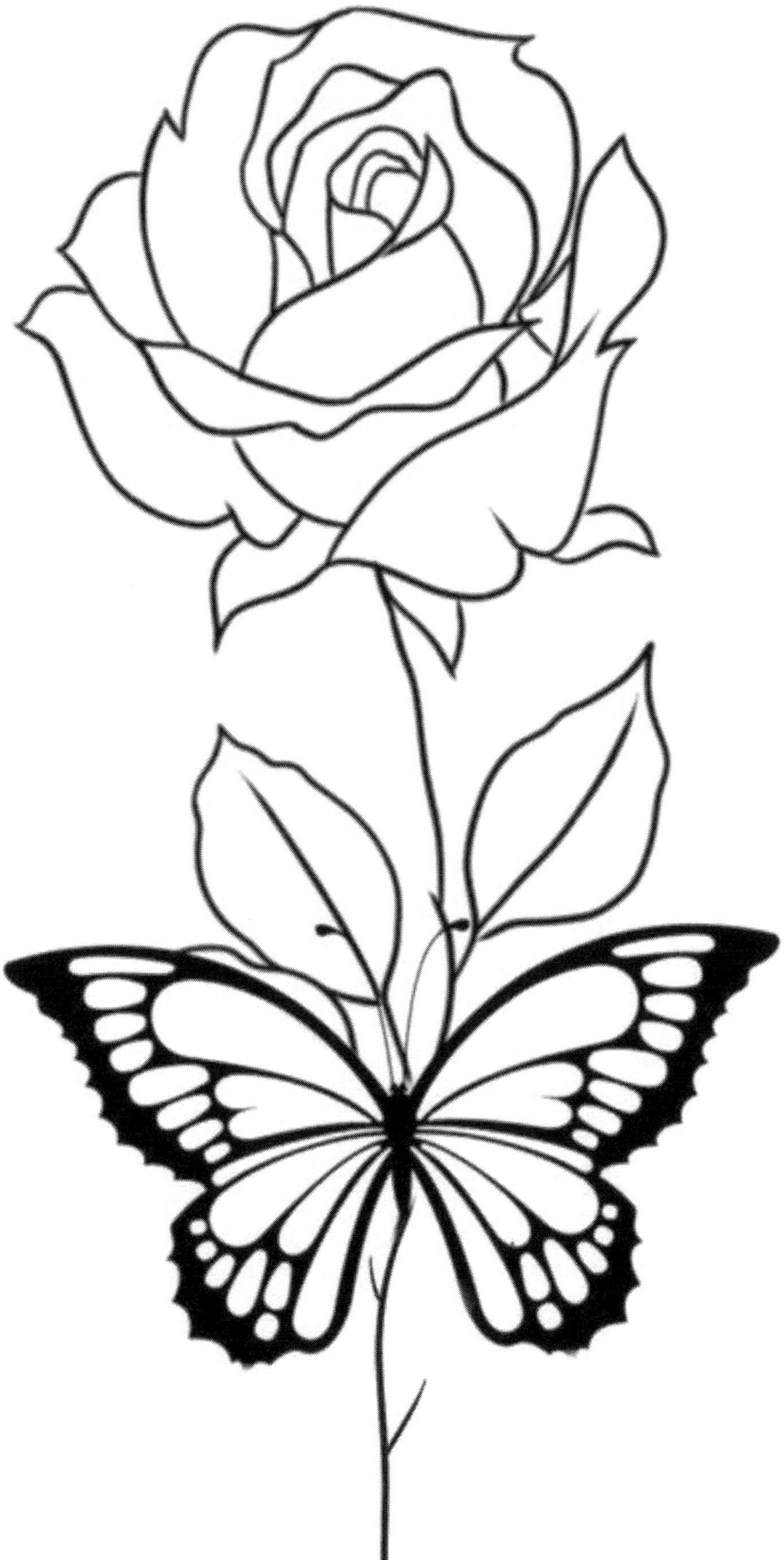

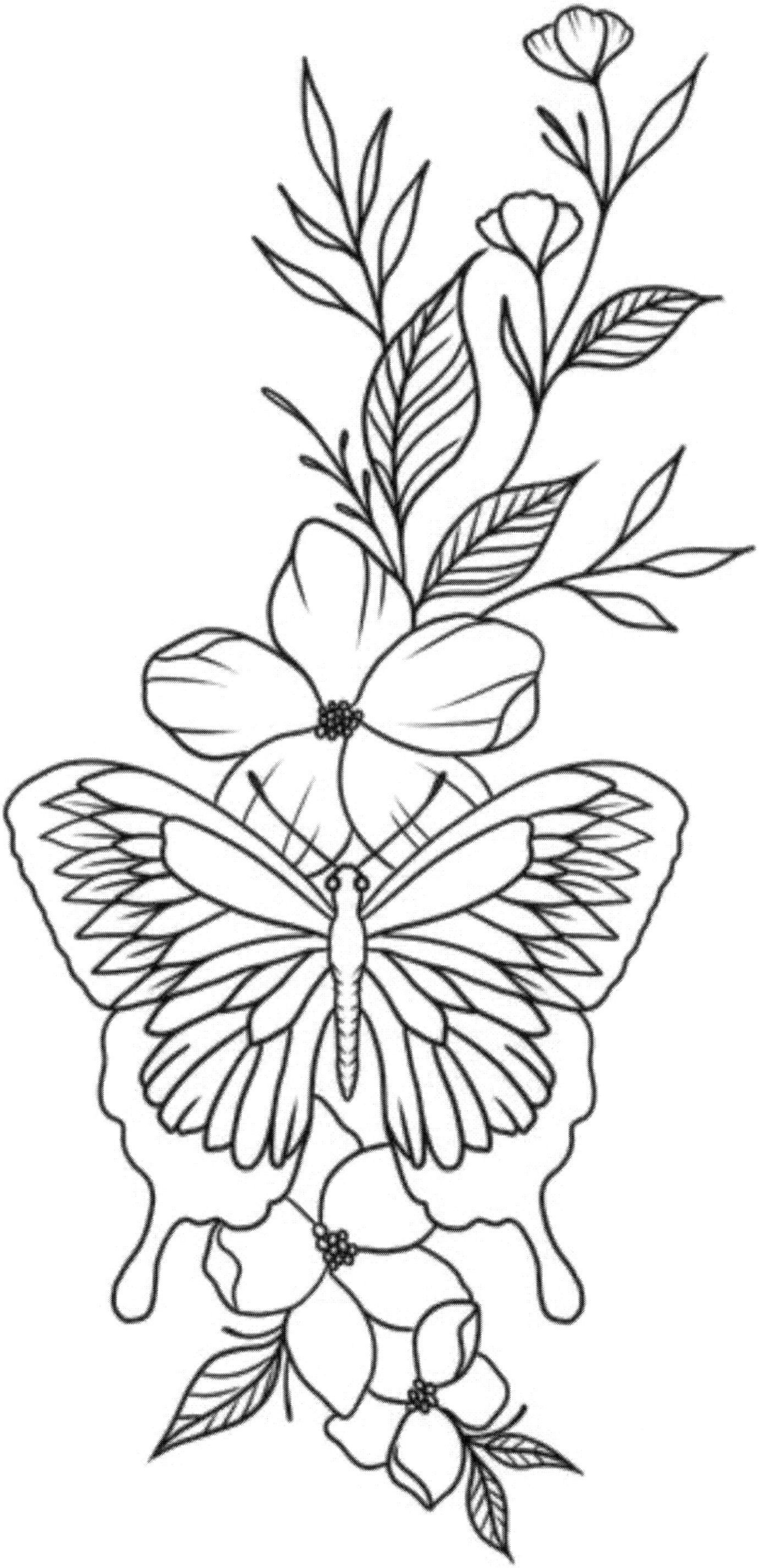

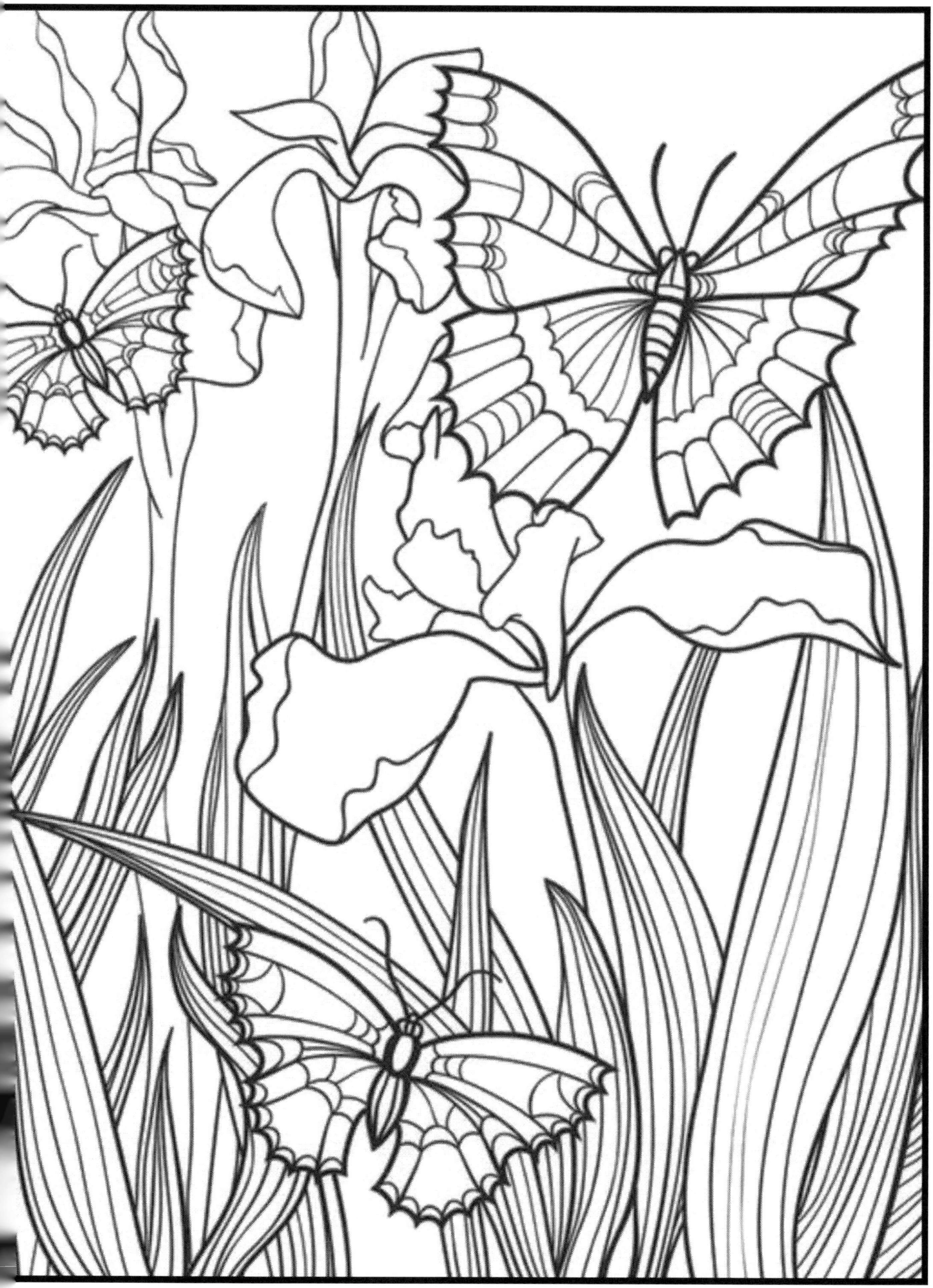

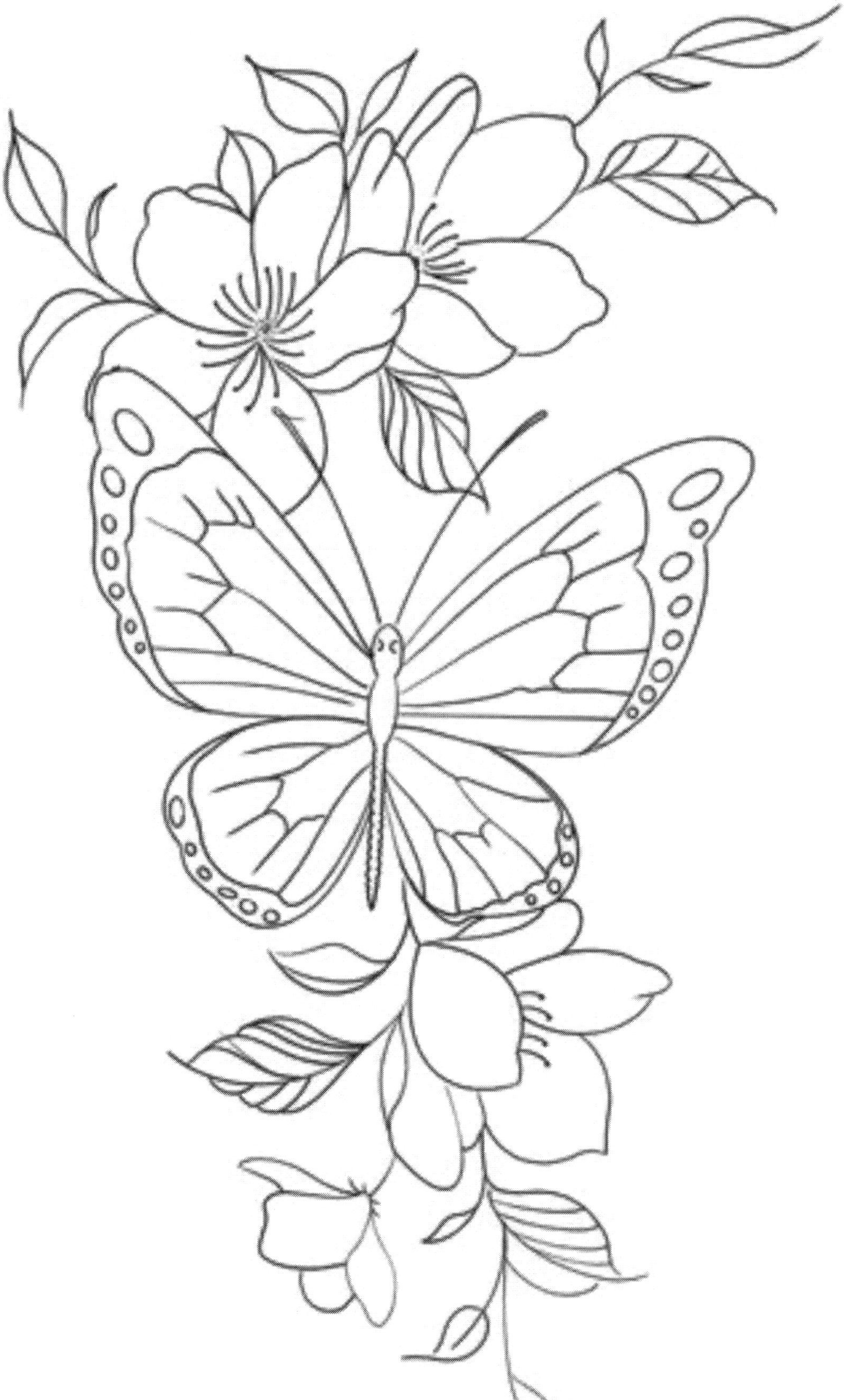

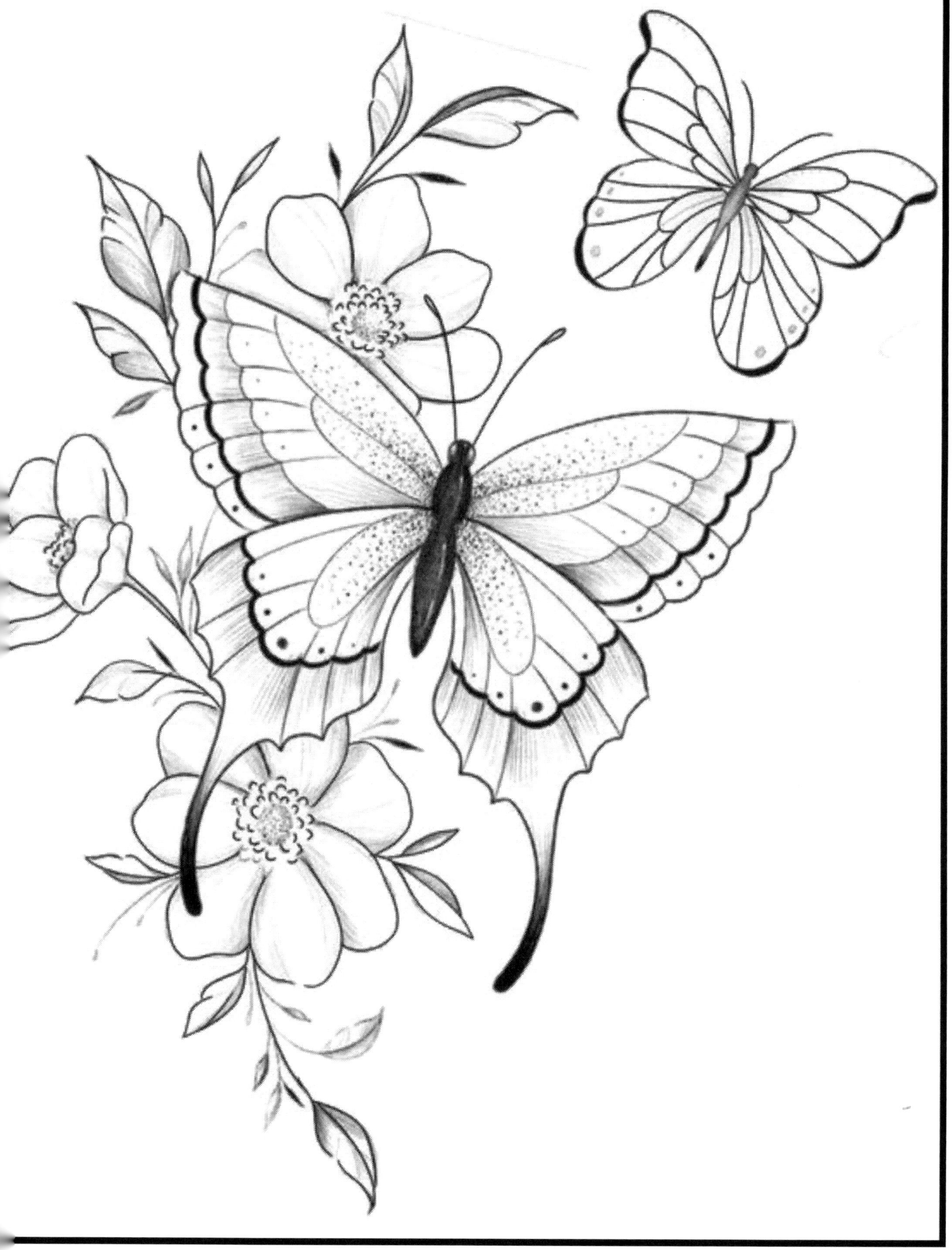

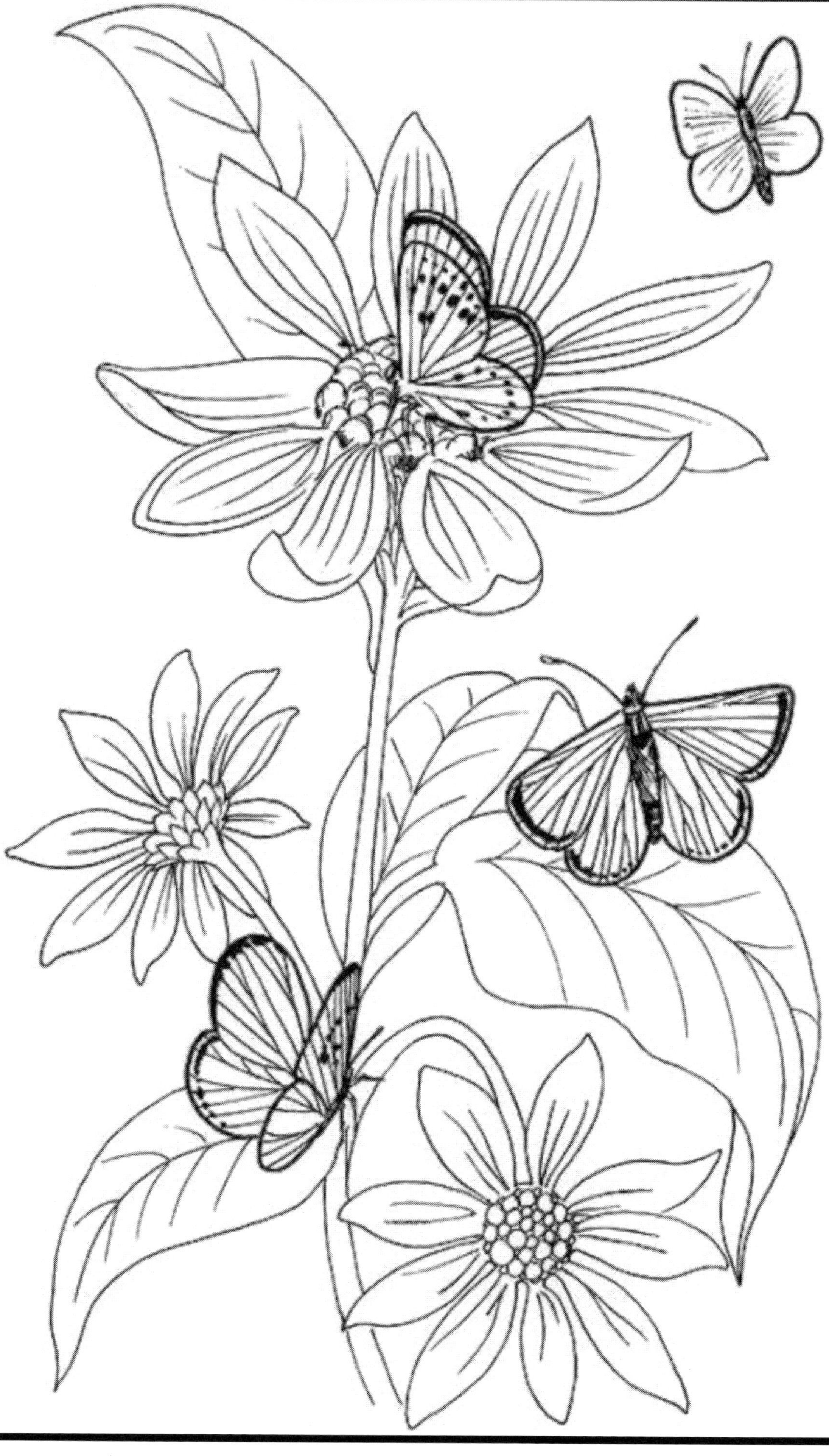

Made in United States
Orlando, FL
18 February 2023

30114126R00057